# Contents

Foreword     5

Introduction     7

Section 1    **The History of the English Mummers' Play:**     **11**

     What Are Mummers?     11

     Origins     15

     Heyday and decline     19

     Mummers today     21

Section 2    **The Mummers and their Performance**     **25**

     Names     25

     Times of performance     27

     Types of play and their distribution     28

     1 The hero-combat play     30

     2 The wooing, bridal or recruiting sergeant play     32

     3 The sword dance play     34

     Characters     35

     Performers     39

     Performance style     41

     Costumes     45

     Venues     48

     Attitudes and motives     49

Section 3    **A Guide to Performance**     **55**

     Getting started     55

     Choosing a text     57

     Casting     59

     Costumes     60

     Props     63

     Performance     67

Section 4    **Sources of Information**     **71**

     Finding Material     73

Section 5    **Play Texts**     **75**

     **Acknowledgements**     **119**

# Room, Room, Ladies and Gentlemen ...

an introduction to the
**English Mummers' Play**

**by Eddie Cass and Steve Roud**
Edited by Malcolm Taylor and Doc Rowe

*In association with The Folklore Society*
*2002*

published by the English Folk Dance and Song Society
In association with The Folklore Society
Copyright © Eddie Cass and Steve Roud 2002
Illustrations and photographs provided by Doc Rowe
Book design by Bryan Ledgard, Ledgard Jepson Ltd.

*Above: "A Party of Mummers" from Chambers' Book of Days, 1864. Courtesy Doc Rowe collection*

 English Folk Dance and Song Society,
Cecil Sharp house, 2 Regent's Park Road,
London NW1 7AY

The Folklore Society,
The Warburg Institute, Woburn Square,
London WC1H 0AB

ISBN 0 85418 185

# Foreword

When I was young, my father told me about the Mummers. They came every New Year. They would knock on the front door and were welcomed into the house. Always strangers, always men, they would come in humming. They had blackened faces and hands, wore dark clothing and carried brooms, and would go through the whole house symbolically sweeping and all the while humming. When they were finished they would leave, not a word spoken, no money changing hands, but leaving gifts of a piece of coal and a piece of bread.

My father neither sought nor offered any explanation for this 'ritual'. This was unusual for him as he was a teacher and always sought an explanation and understanding for everything (indeed, he used to delight in embarrassing doctors by insisting that they translate their impressive sounding Latin names into English!) But this was tradition: to be accepted and respected just as it was - and no questions asked. Clearly, the Mummers and their annual visit enriched his life.

Although my father's mysterious visitors did not speak, this book is about the plays associated with such groups of characters who were once found performing all over the country at certain times of the year. These Mummers and their plays are part of a rich and diverse pattern of traditions still being enacted all over Britain to this very day.

As a young man I joined the Darlington Mummers and learned a great deal from my mentors who had collected and studied Mummers' plays from all parts of England. We thought it important to respect these traditions, which had been handed down from generation to generation. We considered ourselves the temporary custodians of a heritage and our respect for it meant a faithful reproduction of both the words of the plays and how they were performed, including the costumes used. For us, the term 'living tradition'

*Minstead Mummers, Hampshire, by Sir Benjamin Stone*

meant that while we would attempt to faithfully reproduce and hand on each play as we had learnt it, some things would inevitably be changed. Such is the nature of tradition.

In performance, it was both challenging and rewarding to achieve audience response whilst working with these finely honed texts. Performing the plays well is a surprisingly subtle art. Resorting to pantomime antics in order to entertain the audience was shunned and considered to be insulting to both the tradition and to our forbears. It was also an unspoken rule that we kept a very low profile before and after performing. It was important to retain the mystery; to appear from nowhere; to perform the play and then disappear without explanation.

Mystery, I suspect, has always been a part of the Mummers' tradition and the plays raise more questions than answers. I will never forget one bitter winter's day in Ripon, watching three aging men performing their play to a virtually empty street. This was tradition in its strictest sense and their glances at the five spectators present left little doubt that they did not like being watched!

The mystique that surrounds Mummers' plays has resulted in considerable debate. This book has been written by two of England's most respected researchers of Mummers' plays who, in turn, approach the subject from differing angles. That is important, as is the fact that their work appears at a time when there are very few publications available on the subject which deal with it in a serious and balanced manner. It will provide you with a comprehensive summary of one of our most interesting and varied of traditional art forms.

Read the book and form your own opinions. But remember, we are the ancestors of tomorrow and have been entrusted with our heritage. Let us respect these traditions and hand them on to enrich the lives of future generations, just as they have enriched ours.

**Phil Wilson** *Strategic Director EFDSS*
November 2001

# Introduction

This book is designed as an introduction to the mummers' play in England - a widespread, fascinating but much misrepresented traditional custom. We hope that it will be useful for anyone interested in the play, whether from a scholarly or practical point of view. The texts found in Section 5 have been chosen not only to illustrate the variety of play types, but also to make available some previously unpublished or inaccessible examples. The early parts of the book are intended to provide a social and historical context for these scripts with the hope that this will add to the reader's or performer's enjoyment of the play.

Writing an introductory book on the mummers' play is more difficult than it might seem. To begin with, traditional customs are notoriously difficult to generalise about and any broad statement should really be hedged around with many exceptions and qualifications. Just about every aspect of the play varied from place to place and from time to time. Secondly, there are few hard and fast definitions to be found in folklore studies and there are few fixed points to which to anchor our argument. To give you a indication of what we mean, not all authorities have agreed that the mummers' play

*Longparish Mummers, Hampshire*

was really a *play* as such, and few if any of the participants called themselves *Mummers*! Furthermore, much of the literature on mummers still being read and relied upon is now considered by most play scholars to be erroneous, for one reason or another. Hence, in an introductory text such as this, the writers feel obliged to say what the play *is not* in addition to attempting to describe exactly what it *is*.

Having described, dissected, analysed and compared all the data to hand, a true sense of the performance, its excitement, its strangeness, the wonder of the people watching, the colour of the costumes, the sound of wooden swords clashing and hob-nailed boots scraping on flagstones, will always be impossible to recreate in a book such as this. Excitement is a strong element in the recorded memories of those that have seen or participated in the plays themselves:

> *But yester-eve, and the mummers were here! They had come striding into the old kitchen, powdering the red brick floor with snow from their barbaric bedizenments; and stamping, and crossing, and declaiming, till all was whirl and riot and shout ...*

In an attempt to provide some understanding of this excitement, we have interspersed the text with quotations from original sources. In the main, these are descriptions of the mummers' play by observers or participants and are from the late nineteenth century and the early twentieth century.

The book has five main sections: the first two sections cover the history, types, content and distribution of mummers' plays; the third section focuses on aspects of contemporary performance as a guide to those readers who might wish to perform a play; the fourth section guides readers to further information; and the final section contains a selection of texts. We hope you find the book both useful and of help in the understanding of one our most intriguing customary practices.

*Top: Overton Mummers, Hampshire c1930*

*Left: Chithurst Tipteers, Sussex 1900*

**Section 1** # The **History** of the English Mummers' Play

## What are **mummers'**?

**Hampshire Mummers:** *It was the day after Christmas Day, 1891. I had come down from London to spend the Christmas at a farmhouse situated on the high ground which stretches from near Salisbury towards Romsey. There had been frost, and, during the night, a heavy fall of snow. It was a brilliant morning, the sky cloudless and blue, the sun shining on the glistening and sparkling expanse before me, over and beyond the village of Sherfield English to the New Forest....The situation and the scene held me spellbound, when presently I saw moving through the defiles of white undulations in the view before me, coming up from the direction of the village, what at first looked like a gorgeously coloured rope. Presently this appeared as a file of moving figures, attired in all the colours of the rainbow. On they came in the direction of the house wherein I stood, and I was about to seek out my host to enquire as to the meaning of the extraordinary spectacle I had witnessed, when I heard a loud knocking at the kitchen door. Going in the direction of the sound, I encountered members of the family and guests flying down the stairs and through the hall, excitedly exclaiming to each other "The Mummers! The Mummers have come!". Entering the kitchen with the others, there before me, erect and silent, in single file as they had come, but facing inwards to the room, I beheld the figures now disguised in every variety of colours, whose ascent through the snowy scene I had watched from the window. In silence they waited till every sound was still, and then they began and went through their performance. Each in turn left*

*Left: Hampshire Mummer*
*Photo: George Long*
*(courtesy Doc Rowe Collection)*

> *the file of standing figures, announced himself "In comes I, so-and-so" and when his part was finished resumed his place in the row of standing figures. Unrecognisable through the streamers which depended from their headgear, these lads of the village enacted mystery throughout....*
> **[T.F. Ordish, 'Survival in Folk-Lore', *Herne Bay Press* 23rd December, 1922]**

All over Britain, mostly but not always at Christmas time, it was once customary for groups of men to get together to perform their version of a mumming play. They would perform this play over and over again around their neighbourhood for as long as the season lasted and the play would ostensibly be the same each year. They were the *mummers*, or whatever local name they went by. In the villages of rural England, the group of men would normally be the same each year, too, and would usually be the only ones to perform the play. No one else would dream of doing it, although there are instances of more than one team going out, which could lead to some local argument. A second team might also occur where a junior version would be formed specifically to learn and perpetuate the custom.

In the urban areas of industrial England, however, where the performers were often children or young men (half-timers), multiple teams were more likely, but each would perform the play within what local custom accepted as its own home area, sometimes being limited to just a few streets. In addition, the performers would only take part in the play whilst they were of the accepted age category, and would cease to take part thereafter. The play was in some respects recognised as a rite of passage.

'Custom' is a good word to describe this activity as this suggests continuity within the community and an unofficial but locally agreed sanctioning of a practice. Mumming plays are therefore *folklore*. They are part of the traditional, unofficial culture of Britain, which is passed on from person to person both horizontally (geographically) and vertically (over time, from generation to generation). Well over fifteen hundred places in Britain are known to have had a local version of a play and there are probably many others that have not so far been recorded.

It is notoriously difficult to generalise about customary activities. On the one hand they tend to be *conservative*. This is to say that in the regular day-to-day tension between attempting to replicate exactly what one was taught and the need or desire for innovation or creativity, the former usually wins. On the other hand, change certainly does occur. For example, a participant might decide to do or wear something different one year, or a character in a play might be dropped because there were not enough people to complete the 'cast', or a line or two would be forgotten, or an incomer might add something from elsewhere. And so on. Change could be gradual or instant, minor or major, deliberate or not even noticed - but change there certainly was.

Taking all such factors into account, we can regard each local version of a mummers' play, even each performance of that version, as truly unique. Such fluidity within a tradition is one of the most fascinating aspects of folklore, whilst posing problems for researchers. What is more, each person who has come into contact with a piece of folklore and left a record of it, will invariably have introduced a personal perspective. For example, to one observer a mummers' play may be a quaint old survival to be encouraged, while to another it is an excuse for drinking and begging or terrorising the neighbourhood! Each will describe the practice in a very different way and there has been much speculation as to what the play is all about ... especially its origins.

*From* 'Christmas and its Associations' *by W. F. Dawson*

# Origins

Today, most folklorists focus their interest on the social environment in which a custom is performed, rather than on where and when it began. That has not always been the case and folklorists in the past were readier to speculate on the origins of customs about which they read or wrote. The present-day audiences for customary events, on the other hand, are always fascinated by the possible origins of the customs that they are witnessing and expect clear and certain answers to their inevitable questions. Moreover, any answer which appeals in some manner to an earlier period of history or to an assumed concept of 'Merrie England', tends to evoke a deep-seated response. Hence, given that folklorists today are unwilling to provide simplistic answers, the gap is filled by the work of popular writers who are willing to state that most traditional customs, rhymes, superstitions and so on, are relics of pagan rituals and beliefs that are thousands of years old. Unfortunately, such writing is often based on the theories of this earlier generation of folklorists whose research might not have been as rigorous as it should have been. Indeed, it is now generally regarded as marred by an ahistorical approach to the subject, with a tendency to jump to conclusions without hard evidence.

As far as the mummers' play is concerned, these origin theories usually include the following elements:

- It is a survival of a *pre-Christian* ritual.
- It is a *fertility* rite.
- The death and resurrection part of the play is *sympathetic magic* to ensure the return of the sun/summer/etc. each year.
- The characters thus *symbolise* light/dark, good/evil, etc.

The first thing to note here is that the last three elements listed are, in effect, implicitly reliant on the first one. It is only by accepting that the play - or at least the core of the play - is *very, very old* that the other ideas are at all credible. Who would argue that fertility rituals were being *started* at a later date? And it is their survival which is being claimed.

However, the first concrete evidence for a play with a text recognisable as our mumming play dates from the second half of the eighteenth century. Researchers are gradually turning up further 'early' material on the mumming plays and there is a growing cluster of references to recognisable Hero-Combat plays from around the 1720s to the 1750s. But research into the history of the mumming play before the eighteenth century has failed to produce any reliable evidence. In this period there are plenty of references to other customs involving dancing, singing, Maying, visiting, etc., and numerous 'players' and even a few `mummers', but no evidence of any of the plays under discussion here. Hence, what seems increasingly likely is that this early eighteenth century period - or perhaps even the late seventeenth century - will prove to be the point of origin for our play. If that suggestion is correct, then an origin in the wider popular culture of the period looks most likely. Fertility, sympathetic magic, symbols of light and darkness are thus increasingly unlikely. Indeed, the death-resurrection motif turns up in numerous other popular culture contexts (including games and mountebanks' performances designed to sell patent medicines) and is certainly not confined to 'ritual' performance.

Mumming play texts are fascinating in themselves because even in cold print they hold a strange evocative power which is uniquely their own. Nevertheless, for the scholar they pose problems because they are clearly a pastiche of styles, periods and sources which can often be recognised but not identified. To begin with, the presentation of the play has echoes of Elizabethan drama with its call for 'room'. Further, St. George's exploits are based on (but not quoted directly from) earlier sources such as Kirke's *Seven Champions of Christendom*, a text which, in addition to being published in book form, was circulated widely in chapbook format and remained a children's favourite until the early years of the twentieth century. Finally, the Doctor's boasts appear in popular songs and broadsides of the seventeenth and eighteenth centuries, and also in a version of *The Siege of Troy*, a play which was supposedly seen in a fairground booth in Bristol in 1770, whilst various bits of other stage plays pop up in individual texts, and other parts have parallels in children's games.

It should be noted that identifiable literary borrowings occur in only a handful of versions of the play and therefore tell us little. But it is all too easy to oversimplify and construct an attractive argument for origins from such a slender a record of evidence. For example, at Overton and North Waltham (Hampshire), the whole gang sings:

> *He comes, he comes, Oh here Oh here he comes*
> *Sound, sound the trumpets and beat Oh beat the dreams*
> *It's from shore to shore along the cannons roar*
> *Walk in King George along the British shore*

These words can be compared with the lines from Thomas Morell's libretto first used for Handel's oratorio *Joshua* (1748):

> *See the conquering hero comes*
> *Sound the trumpets, beat the drums*
> *Sports prepare, the laurel bring*
> *Songs of triumph to him sing*

This does not mean that Handel wrote the mumming play, but it does reinforce our understanding of the readiness with which mummers of the past were willing to draw on the whole range of popular culture for their texts. This eclecticism supports the view that we are unlikely to find one single proto-text for a mumming play. During the period in which we believe the mumming play came into use, the working or labouring class drew their literary culture from a number of sources, both oral and written (e.g. chapbooks and broadsides), and importantly from the plays and interludes of the booth theatres which were a feature of every fair from the medieval period until the late nineteenth century. These were not discrete sources but media which interacted. The actors of booth theatres could draw on chapbooks and broadsides for their scripts, which in turn could influence the content of printed material as well as forming an essential part of oral culture. It is within this complex nexus that the mumming play probably emerged, but did so and spread in a way we do not yet, and perhaps never will, fully comprehend.

Folklorists of the past, such as life-cycle theorists Alex Helm and Margaret Dean-Smith, felt able to dismiss the texts as relatively meaningless 'accretions' and to concentrate on the *action* of the play, which they saw as the oldest and most important element . That is, the death and resurrection, or the wooing, depending on your viewpoint:

> *"My first proposition is that the Play, and any significance it may have, resides in the action: the text is a local accretion, often both superfluous and irrelevant. The Play can exist in action alone, without a word spoken..."*
> **Margaret Dean-Smith, The Life-Cycle or Folk Play',**
> **Folklore Vol.69 (1958) pp.237-253.**

The extension of this idea – that the words of the play are simply grafted on to an already existing luck-visit ritual – again falls at the first hurdle. There is no evidence for a death-resurrection custom in Britain before the rise of the mumming play.

Today, however, scholars see the text of the mumming play as being as important as the script of any other play. For those researchers who are as interested in the development and spread of the plays as in their origin, and who further wish to understand more about their traditional performance and context, the texts obviously contain vital clues - if we could just learn how to read them! The work of people such as Baskervill and Chambers, who attempted to find literary parallels to parts of the texts of mumming plays, went out of fashion with the rise of Alex Helm's generation. However, they left an invaluable corpus of evidence identifying a number of analogues in popular drama and literature of the past. No systematic work has followed up their lead, but such work in the future may tell us a great deal about the transmission of texts and, perhaps, their history and origin(s).

# **Heyday** and decline

Although the mummers' play started entering the documentary record in the eighteenth century, it is during the nineteenth century that references increase dramatically. This is not necessarily a true reflection of the popularity of the custom, but possibly a function of the increasing interest in folklore on the part of educated observers and the growth of local newspapers. On the other hand, it has been argued that the rise and spread of chapbook versions of the mumming play from the mid-nineteenth century may have had an impact on the transmission and performance of the play. A more verifiable indicator of the popularity of the custom may be a decline in the number of recorded performances in the last years of the nineteenth century - and the tone of the writers who tended to bemoan the passing of the old ways.

Certainly, one major watershed was the First World War. Not only did many of the mummers fail to return from the War, but many of those who survived or were left behind did not have the heart to revive the custom, particularly where previous participants were conspicuous by their absence. Shifts in society in general were also taking their toll on customs, most potently the progressive decline of rural areas and the rise of other forms of entertainment, such as the radio, cinema, dance halls and professional sport. Moreover, the paternalism which had been part of the economic and social culture of both rural and urban England, began to decline from the 1880s onwards. This led to a changing attitude towards what many then construed as begging. There was also an unwillingness on the part of young people to follow in the footsteps of their parents, who were also discovering the attraction of some of the new forms of entertainment. Ex-mummers recorded in the 1970s and 1980s have described such trends as instrumental in the decline of mumming after the Great War.

Nevertheless, there were still many extant teams in the 1920s and 1930s, probably in the order of three or four hundred nation-wide, but their numbers gradually dwindled and only a handful were left after the Second World War. By about 1950 several of these teams had ceased to perform, and in England today just six teams have

any credible claims to a history dating back beyond the 1940s: Marshfield (Gloucestershire), Antrobus (Cheshire), Midgley (Yorkshire), Bampton (Oxfordshire), Uttoxeter (Staffordshire) and Symondsbury (Dorset).

## Mummers **today**

The majority of mumming plays performed today are by groups which were formed out of the post-Second World War folk revival movement. Many of these teams have been performing for thirty years or more and have clearly established themselves as traditional performers in their own area. These groups fall into at least two different categories.

The first, and probably least numerous, are groups such as the Bradshaw Mummers and the Knaresborough Mummers, both of Yorkshire, and the Coventry Mummers of Warwickshire. These groups see themselves as 'semi-professional' in that instead of performing a local play in one town or village, they perform a variety of plays at venues such as folk festivals. In the case of the Coventry Mummers, much of their material is drawn from traditional texts from different parts of the country, whereas both the Knaresborough Mummers and the Bradshaw team write much of their own material, and, in the case of the latter group, their performances can include elaborate stage effects. Whilst the performances of these last groups can sometimes be a far cry from those recorded in the past, such groups can be seen as descendants of the mediaeval *jongleur* tradition, which may well have played a part in the eighteenth and nineteenth century development of mumming plays.

In contrast to the first group, there are other teams who seek to work in an older mode. Such a team is the Bury Pace-Eggers of Lancashire who took a known nineteenth century text from their own area and tried to re-establish the play within the tradition in which it was originally performed. Pace-egging has had a long history in Lancashire, the first reference dating from 1820 in the Bury area. The team has sought to accurately recreate the play, insofar as this is possible to establish. The costumes which the team wear are

*Marshfield Paper Boys*

created from the information contained in the book in which the text was set down, and supplemented by information which Alan Seymour, the team leader, gleaned from his own research into the play. The style of performance is similarly traditionally based with the actors declaiming their lines rather than trying to 'act' the part. There is some humour in the play but there is no attempt to overplay this aspect. Other contemporary mummers have not always kept so strictly to the older manner of performance and have added to texts, sometimes substantially. Alternatively, they may have developed a manner of acting which is at variance with the way in which plays might have been performed in the past, sometimes drawing on pantomime, the music hall or street theatre in devising their performance style.

Many of today's plays do not have the deep roots in a small community that they may have had in the past, particularly in the years prior to the First World War. Also, instead of being enacted by performers from a working-class background, we now have plays by middle-class folk enthusiasts who perform them for reasons which may differ greatly from those of their predecessors. However, when discussing these post-war plays, we should perhaps take account of what it is that present day mummers believe that they are doing. Whilst some present day mummers may be happy to perform a range of earlier plays as itinerant players at folk festivals, this is not always the case. Many pace-eggers in Lancashire, for example, are very clear that they are continuing an Easter tradition which has a recorded history of nearly 200 years in the county. They see themselves acting out a customary drama within a countywide tradition, and one which, in some places at least, was performed within living memory. They, and their fellow mummers in other parts of the country, are essentially seeking to perpetuate a valued customary performance, and in a way which might resonate with the motives of participants in other customary events in England today.

*Top: School Mummers, Abingdon, Oxfordshire*

*Right: Midgley Pace Egg Play. Calder Valley*

## Section 2 **The Mummers** and their performance

### Names

Writers usually refer to the custom as *mumming* and the performers as *mummers*, but although these words were understood by participants (at least in the twentieth century), the mummers themselves had their own local or regional terms, such as *Tipteerers* (Sussex / Surrey) *Johnny* or *Jolly Jacks* (Hampshire), *Pace-Eggers* (Lancashire / Yorkshire), *White Boys* (Isle of Man), *Christmas Boys* (Isle of Wight), *Plough Jags* (Lincolnshire) and *Soul Cakers* (Cheshire).

Some of these names are relatively straightforward, determined by a particular character in the play (e.g. Johnny Jack), the play's time of appearance (e.g. Christmas Boys) or the costumes used (e.g. White Boys, Paper Boys). Some, however, have defied all attempts at etymology, such as *Tipteerers*. When asked, the performers have usually been puzzled by such questions - "Tipteerers are people who go Tipteering, of course!" and vice versa! The term *mumming* has itself caused some difficulties for commentators. Most point out the similarity with the Old Danish for `masking' and thus presume a Teutonic origin for the custom. The term also has various historical connections with 'acting', 'miming', etc. It is possible, however, that the word has been imposed on the custom by the educated collectors over the years and therefore provides no real clue to the history of the tradition.

*Left: Nettley Abbey, Hampshire, 1892 from The Ordish Collection, The Folklore Society*

**Cumbrian Jollyboys**: *Sir - I have read with great interest the correspondence about Jolly Boys, more so as I was one of a troop in the early 80's of last century at Hesket-New-Market [Cumberland]. I started as Bessie Brown Bags the Miser, and rose through the various characters till I arrived at King George, resplendent in a paper cocked hat with small streamers, and a red coat with belt and sword. Lord Nelson was dressed likewise, only his hat was worn crosswise. Dr. Brown (Jolly Jack Tar) wore a black topper hat, black swallow-tailed coat and white waistcoat; Tosspot had his coat turned wrong side out and face blacked, and the miser wore any old rags, more torn the better. Before singing the song ...we acted the play. During the four or five years that I was a Jolly Boy, we were only ordered out of a house once. We visited all the farms and gentlemen's houses (no cottages) in a radius of five miles, and were invariably welcomed with pleasure, especially if there were children. To them, the Jolly Boys were a delight and something to look forward to. I would like to see the play and song revived again.*
**[John Jackson, Cumberland & Westmorland Herald
8th March, 1952]**

Below: Goathland
Plough Stots,
Goathland, North
Yorkshire

# **Times** *of performance*

Invariably, mummers had a particular time of year at which they performed and would not normally appear at any other times - which is why mumming plays are termed *calendar* or *seasonal* customs by folklorists. There are isolated examples, however, of teams performing at special occasions, such as the Festival of Britain, coronation celebrations, local fetes, and so on, but this is unusual. The time of year varies from region to region, but is always in the winter period between Hallowe'en and Easter. However, by far the most common season for mumming throughout the country is around Christmas and New Year - starting in mid-December and continuing to the beginning of January.

> **Gloucestershire Mummers**: *When I was a child at Dumbleton Rectory, I used to look forward greatly to the visit of the mummers at Christmas, when I was allowed to sit on the kitchen table drawn aside for the purpose, and thus to watch them. All the year our old nurse used to collect and put by bits of lace and ribbon for them, with which to decorate their tall conical caps with long streamers. As far back as 1879 I took down the actual words of their mumming ...*
>
> **[Miss Wedgwood, in Evesham Journal**
> **23rd December, 1939, p.2]**

# **Types of play** and their distribution

Anyone looking through a number of mumming play texts will recognise their marked similarity, both over time (the past 260 years) and space (almost all over the British Isles and a few places abroad as well). A superficial analysis of all the information we now have on mummers' traditions clearly shows that, on the whole, the tradition is regional - that is, plays which have been collected from locations close to each other are more similar than those from places further apart. It is thus possible, in the broadest sense, to write of a particular version as being typical (or untypical) of an area or region with regard to a particular aspect - whether it be costume, text, character-names, and so on. A closer look, however, inevitably presents a much more confused picture. Not only do the 'regions' have jagged edges and areas of overlap, but there are numerous and puzzling anomalies.

There are basically three types of play, given here in order of frequency of occurrence. This three-fold classification is based, with some modifications, on that described by Cawte, Helm & Peacock in *English Ritual Drama*.

*Left: Dick, the Wild Horse from Antrobus Soulcakers Play, Cheshire*

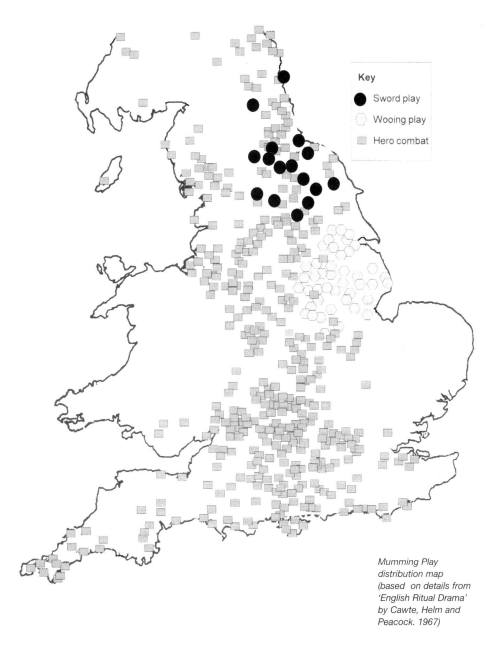

Key

● Sword play

⬡ Wooing play

▨ Hero combat

*Mumming Play
distribution map
(based on details from
'English Ritual Drama'
by Cawte, Helm and
Peacock. 1967)*

# 1 The hero-combat play

This type is often called the *St. George play* after its most common
character. The play is usually described as having a number of
elements: the presentation or introduction, the vaunt or boast, the
combat, the lament, the cure and the *quête*, a term with which
Chambers described the final part of the play with its associated
collection. Simply summarised, an introduction is followed by a
character (e.g. St. George) who boasts of his prowess and
challenges someone (or all-comers) to a fight. Another character
(e.g. Turkish Knight) takes up the challenge. They fight and one is
wounded or killed. Someone laments the death and a doctor is
called. The doctor (or his assistant) cures or revives the
dead/wounded man. A succession of supernumerary characters
appears, each reciting some lines and in some cases performing
some short action. At least one of these characters requests money,
food, drink, etc. In many versions, the combat is repeated with
different characters and in some plays there may be more than one
cure.

Three sub-groups of the hero-combat play have been identified,
although further intensive regional studies of the play may identify
additional sub-groups. The first group is the *souling play,* confined to
parts of Cheshire and performed primarily around All Souls Day, as
is the Galoshins play in some parts of Scotland. It should be noted
here that there is also a singing and begging custom in Cheshire,
without a play, called *souling*. This is not to be confused with the
souling song which the actors sing as part of their performance. The
play also includes a performance by a Wild Horse character and its
driver. The Wild Horse comes in at the end of the play and provides
much entertainment for the audience.

**Cheshire Soulcakers:** *In Cheshire the Hobby Horse (known
here as the Wild Horse) comes in at the end of the play and he
and his driver introduce a 'turn', to use a music-hall term, which
is quite independent of the play; but the Wild Horse capers and
the narration of its adventures are always regarded as the high
spot of the entertainment. An actual horse's skull is painted in
traditional colours, its jaws are made to work and snap, and it is*

*supported on a pole by a man who is covered with a rug and
who thus makes the hind legs of a three-legged horse. These
heads are held in high esteem; one owned by the Antrobus
gang has been in use for over 100 years ...*

**[A.W. Boyd, A Country Parish: Great Budworth in the
County of Chester (London: Collins, 1951) pp.68-76]**

The second sub-group is the *Pace-Egg play*, performed at Easter in
Lancashire and in parts of the surrounding counties. The text of the
pace-egg play includes somewhat distinctive characters and, as in
the nearby souling play tradition, the performance includes the
singing of a pace-egg song. Likewise, there are several other
customs known in the north west of England as pace-egging which
do not include a play.

The final sub-group is the Robin Hood play, distinguished by the
presence of Robin Hood as a character and some lines of text
based on two Robin Hood ballads [for these plays, see Michael J.
Preston, 'The Robin Hood Folk Plays of South-Central England',
*Comparative Drama* Vol.10 (1976) pp.91-100]. This is by far the
rarest of the three.

The Hero-Combat is the most widespread of the three types of
mummers' play. Hundreds of versions have been noted from almost
all over England, with the only completely blank counties being
Norfolk, Suffolk and Cambridgeshire, although Essex and
Bedfordshire have only one or two references each. This pattern
may merely be a reflection of where most collecting activity has
been carried out over the years, but the distribution map shows a
definite concentration of locations up the centre of the country –
from Hampshire and Wiltshire, up through Gloucestershire, Berkshire
and Oxfordshire, and spreading across the country as one
progresses north to Cheshire, Lancashire and Yorkshire. Indeed, it is
not uncommon for hero-combats to be found in areas where other
types of play predominate, and even embedded in other types of
play, particularly the wooing plays.

## 2 The wooing, bridal or recruiting sergeant play

This type is also called the *Plough Play* because the usual time of performance was Plough Monday (the first Monday after January 6th) and the teams often carried a plough around with them. The men are thus called Plough Jags or Plough Stots. Here a man woos a young 'female' but is rejected and then persuaded by a Recruiting Sergeant to enlist in the army. The 'female' then accepts the advances of the Clown or Fool and they agree to marry. An older 'female' enters and accuses the Clown of being the father of her illegitimate child, which he denies. Two characters fight, one is killed or wounded and is revived by a Doctor. Much of the play is expressed in song. Men always played the 'female' parts.

Commentators have tended to classify all 'wooing' plays together, but recently Peter Millington has argued convincingly for two distinct but overlapping types [see Peter Millington, 'The Plough Boy and the Plough Play...' *Folk Music Journal* 7:1 (1995) pp.71-72)]. In the first type, the 'female' already has a suitor (the Farmer's Man) who is then persuaded to enlist by a Recruiting Sergeant. She then accepts

*Below: Yorkshire Plough Stots (Doc Rowe Collection)*

the Fool's advances. Millington calls this type 'The Recruiting Sergeant Play'. In the second, the 'female' is wooed by a succession of suitors, which she rejects and finally chooses the Fool. Millington suggests 'Multiple Wooing Play' as a name for this type. It is the multiple wooing play which appears first in documentary record, from the 1820s onwards, but the Recruiting Sergeant Play that was much more common.

Wooing plays of either description were found only in the East Midlands - Lincolnshire, Nottinghamshire, Leicestershire and Rutland [see C.R. Baskervill, 'Mummers' Wooing Plays in England', *Modern Philology* Vol.21 (1923) pp.225-172 for the early Multiple Wooing texts, and *Folk-Lore* Vol.50 (1939) pp.88-97 for two Recruiting Sergeant texts]

> **The Plough Jags**: *The good old custom was kept upon Monday and Tuesday when gangs of youths and young men dressed in fantastic and dazzling attire came `Plough Jagging'. The Soldier, The Lady, and tall hat men, along with the Hobby Horses, attracted considerable attention as they paraded the principal streets, and solicited subscriptions. The time for carrying `The Plough' and pulling up scrapers in order to vent their wrath and fury if refused money has gone by, and the youngsters appear to be on much more familiar terms with the `Plough Boys' than they used to be. The best gang this year hailed from West Halton.*
> **[Lindsey & Lincolnshire Star 11th January, 1902, p.5]**

# 3 The sword dance play

This play is confined to Yorkshire, Durham and Northumberland and
performed in conjunction with linked sword-dances. Versions from
some villages, such as Ampleforth in North Yorkshire, have extensive
texts, whilst others are more vestigial. At some point in the
performance of the dance, a lock of swords is placed around a
man's neck and he is 'killed'. A Doctor, a Clown, or a `Female' then
revives him. It is debatable whether the play accompanies the
dance, or vice versa. There are many places that have a sword
dance tradition without a play, and it is not known whether these
have lost their play or have always been thus unencumbered.
Whatever the case, the sword dance play is the rarest of the three
types and many play scholars consider that the evidence for its
independent existence is the least satisfactory.

> **The Sword Dancers** - *According to Mrs. Keith, Guisers and
> Sword Dancers are closely akin. "Almost the first thing I can
> remember was when we lived at the Dovecot, and Sword
> Dancers came at New Year, in the dark, and danced the sword
> dance in the back yard by the light of lanterns, all dressed up, -
> there was old Betty, and Nelson, and a Doctor, and after they'd
> finished the dance one held up all the swords. They came from
> about Boghall. Yes, miners and the lads about. They used to
> come from Blaydon too. They were given ginger wine, and
> cake".*
>
> **[Rosalie E. Bosanquet, *In the Troublesome Times:
> Memories of Old Northumberland
> Collected by the Cambo Women's Institute*
> (Newcastle: Northumberland Press, 1929) pp.22-23]**

# Characters

There are three main facets to any play characters: what they say, what they do and what they are called. Although each mumming play has no more than a handful of characters, well over 700 individual character names have been identified in play texts. In view of such an extensive list of potential characters, it would be difficult to present any meaningful list. The following description, therefore, is merely a simplified look at some common characters appearing in the mummers' plays, categorised firstly by their actions (i.e. their basic role in the play) and then by their name.

## 1  Hero-combat
### The Presentation or opening of the play

In many plays, the presenter is not named, or is given as **First Man**, **Presenter**, **Leading Man**, **Foreman** or **Headman.** It is not clear whether this is a *name* or merely a description for the purpose of text transcription. Another common presenter is **Bold Roomer**, whose name varies considerably (**Captain Room, Room Room, Gallant Roamer**, etc.). Some commentators spell it as Rumour, but he seems to have taken his name from the fact that he calls for *Room* for the performance to take place. He occurs all across the south of England.

**Father Christmas** is one of the most widespread characters, invariably appearing as either the main presenter, or one of the main presenters. He is also usually the one who laments the fallen combatant and calls for and haggles with the Doctor. It should be noted that the Father Christmas of the mumming play bears little resemblance to the character as popularly portrayed today. There is no mention of presents, reindeer, chimneys or children being good with this version of the character, although plenty of food and drink are part of the proceedings. He is more akin to the old 'Father of Christmas' idea:

> *In comes I old Father Christmas*
> *Am I welcome or am I not*
> *I hope old Father Christmas*
> *Will never be forgot*

## **The boasts** and the combat

The first character the Presenter introduces is almost invariably
**Saint George** or **King George**, who is by far the most common
combatant character name across the country even though there
are areas where he appears only rarely or even not at all. His boasts
usually include references to the famous St. George legend - the
dragon, winning a princess, and so on - so it is pretty safe to
assume that as a mummers' character he was a Saint before he
was a King. It also seems fairly certain that the other occasional
English kings or princes, such **King William** or **Prince George**, are
a further and later development. In Scotland and sometimes in
northern England**,** the main combatant is **Galoshins** or **Galatians**.
He is unknown elsewhere, although for some unknown reason he
appears in a text from Devon!

In the play, St. George will be called upon to fight a range of
enemies. One of the most common, the **Turkish Knight**, is often
called **Turkeysnipe**. He is extremely common across the south of
England, but less so in the Midlands, and rarer still in the north.

**Bold Slasher**'s name varies more than St. George or the Turkish
Knight. **Beau Slasher**, **Captain Slasher**, **Cut and Slash** and **Bull
Slasher** are just a few. He is often coupled with a description, which
can be confusing: *'In comes I the Valiant Soldier, Bold Slasher is my
name.'* He is nearly as common a combatant as the Turkish Knight
and found all over England, whereas the **Valiant Soldier**
occasionally appears as a separate character or with another name.

**(Black) Prince of Paradise** appears regularly across Yorkshire,
Lancashire, Derbyshire, Cheshire, and Staffordshire, but rarely
elsewhere. He is often coupled with **Black Morocco King.**

Other characters appearing in this part of the play include the **King
of Egypt,** who is fairly common in the north and west of England,
but much rarer in the south; **Noble Captain**, a common character
name in Sussex, with a few examples in Hampshire, but rare
elsewhere; **Oliver Cromwell**, who is common in Ireland but only
found in one or two scattered places in England; and **Saint Patrick,**
who is again relatively common in Ireland but who makes one or two
appearances in England.

## The cure

After one of the characters has been wounded or killed in the combat, he is cured by the ubiquitous **Doctor** - the single most common character who is found in virtually every play. He is often given a name - Doctor Parr, Doctor Dodd, Doctor Brown, etc which in some cases may be a reference to a local personality, but is probably more often dictated by the rhyme of the following line: *"In comes I old Doctor Brown, best old doctor in this town"*.

The Doctor sometimes has a name which links him with **Jack** or **John Finney** or **Vinney**, or to **Tom**, **Moll** or **Molly**, **Spinney**, **Winney**, **Pinnick**, and so on. This character variation is common across Berkshire, Oxfordshire, Warwickshire and Gloucestershire; rarer in Northamptonshire and Wiltshire; and almost unknown elsewhere. He acts as the Doctor's assistant, or sometimes as the doctor himself, and invariably has humorous or topsy-turvy lines where he cheeks and parodies the Doctor.

## The quête

This part of the play has the widest range of possible participants, of whom **Beelzebub** is probably the most widespread. Beelzebub is an extremely fluid name, occurring as **Belsey Bob**, **Belsie Bug**, **Helsey Bub**, **Alezebub**, and possibly as **Eezum Squeezum**. The name is found all over England:

*In comes I Beelzebub*
*Over my shoulder I carry my club*
*In my hand a dripping pan*
*Don't you think I'm a jolly old man?*

**Little Johnny Jack**, also known as **Little Happy Jack**, **Jolly Jack** and **Saucy Jack,** is very common across the south of England and also known in some parts of the north:

*In comes I little Johnny Jack*
*Wife and family on my back*
*My family's large but I am small*
*Every little helps to feed us all*

**Big Head** appears frequently in the south of England, fairly often in the Midlands, and sometimes in the north. Variations include **Little Wit**, **Fiddler Wit**, **Billy Wit**, **Mazzant Binnit** and **Head Per Nip**. A standardised version of his usual lines would be:

> *In comes I as hasn't been yet*
> *With my big head and little wit*

To complicate the issue, these lines are said by another character in many versions, but the geographical distribution is unchanged.

**Devil Doubt**, often known as **Little Devil Doubt,** or sometimes even **Dairy** or **Derry Doubt,** is a very common *quête* character across the north of England, but rarer in the Midlands and extremely rare in the south:

> *In comes I little Devil Doubt, With my shirt-tail hanging out*
> *If you don't give me money, I'll sweep you all out.*

**Twing Twang** is often combined and confused with Little Johnny Jack and reasonably common across Hampshire and Sussex, occasionally used in Berkshire, Kent and Wiltshire, but unknown elsewhere:

> *In comes I Twing Twang*
> *Head man of this press gang*
> *Come to press all you bold mummers...*

Contrary to popular opinion, the **Dragon** appears very rarely in mumming plays, although there are a few texts, spread across England, where he appears as a speaking character. Considering the geographical spread of these locations, plus the fact that the Dragon's speech in each of these versions is virtually identical, there is strong circumstantial evidence to suggest that all these texts derive directly from a single literary source.

[For further information, see Steve Roud & Craig Fees, `Notes on a Quest for Dragons', *Roomer* Vol. 4 No.6 pp.61-64].

**Robin Hood** - The handful of references (about 20 so far reported) to plays where Robin Hood is a combatant character form a sort of sub-set of the Hero-Combat play. Not all of these references give texts, but where they do the Robin Hood , Little John and Tanner lines are similar, although often garbled. The rest of these versions are fairly normal hero-combat plays. The odd thing is the geographical spread - Berkshire (2), Oxfordshire (2), Gloucestershire (4), Wiltshire (1), Derbyshire (3), Nottinghamshire (2), Yorkshire (1) and Glamorgan, although in the latter the Robin Hood does not have any distinctive lines.

## 2  Wooing or plough play

These plays have many characters, the names of which are the same as those used in the hero-combat plays: **King** or **St. George** and **Slasher** are just two examples. However, others are unique to the group. Of this unique set, two are male characters and two are female characters, but which were, in reality, men dressed as women. The two male characters are **Farmer's Man** and the **Recruiting Sergeant** (or just **Sergeant**), and the female characters are **Old Dame Jane** (otherwise **Dame Jane** or just **Jane)** and **Lady Bright and Gay** (or just **Lady**).

## 3  Sword Dance Play

With such a small number of examples and wide variations, it is not so easy to generalise about the characters of the sword dance play. There is usually a **Fool** or **Clown,** a **King**, a **Queen**, and even when there is no developed play, a **Betty** or other 'female' character. The dancers often have names which are enumerated in the 'Calling-On' song, but they do not normally have parts in the play.

# Performers

Traditionally, the participants in mumming plays were *male*. Even the parts of 'female' characters were played by men or boys. There are isolated references to women taking part, even young girls where children continued the tradition, but in the overwhelming majority of cases it was a male custom. Women, perhaps inevitably, were regularly involved in a support role, such as in the making of costumes, and, of course, in helping the men to remember the words where there had been a break in the tradition.

The age of the performers varied from place to place and probably also changed over time. Many accounts refer to 'young men' or 'youths' as predominating, but there is plenty of evidence for older men also taking part, many of them throughout their entire adult lives. Participation often ran in families, over several generations, with youngsters being introduced into the less onerous parts and working their way up into the main characters. Examples here include the Hardcastle family of Ripon and the Williams' family who still perform the Uttoxeter play each Christmas. Some reports refer to two teams - senior and junior - in the same village. In some urban areas, especially in northern England, the tradition was kept alive by children's teams; some performing regularly year after year and others 'got up' on an ad hoc basis when the opportunity or situation dictated.

Apart from familial connections, performers were often drawn from the same occupation, such as ploughboys on the same farm, fishermen, miners or council workers. In most cases, however, this probably represented existing friendships or neighbourhood links rather than any perceived essential occupational link. In many small communities, of course, family, occupation and residence overlapped and combined in complex networks.

Almost without exception, mumming was a *working* or *labouring class* custom. The local middle class and gentry sometimes viewed such customs with scorn, especially where excessive drinking and horseplay took place, and argued for their suppression. Others, meanwhile, particularly in the late nineteenth century, welcomed the mummers as a link with an increasingly romanticised rural past and encouraged the tradition by regularly allowing them to perform at their homes or by giving them money, food and drink. When the custom lapsed in a particular area, it was sometimes one of local gentry who was instrumental in getting it revived. Violet Alford, for example, was responsible for the revival of the Marshfield play, and A.W. Boyd was a key figure in sustaining the souling play traditions of Cheshire, the Antrobus Gang paying visits to his home in Sevenoaks, Kent, until his death in 1959 [Simon Lichman, 'The Gardener's Story: The Metalfolkore of a Mumming Tradition', *Folklore* 93:1, 1982, pp.105-110; Peter K. Harrop, 'The Performance of English Folk Plays: A Study in Dramatic Form and Social Function', unpublished PhD thesis, University of Leeds, 1980, Chap. 3.]. Such men and women as Alford and Boyd, therefore, had an important role to play in encouraging, supporting and legitimising the custom, but did not actually take part themselves.

## Performance style

A problem with many descriptions of the mummers' play is the inappropriate use of theatrical models for comparison or analysis. Some commentators have dismissed mummers' plays because of the limited plot, the doggerel style text, the lack of acting ability on the part of the performers, and so on. Even on the surface, the traditional mummers' play is different from other plays. To begin with, the same play text (with perhaps one or two minor changes) was performed at the same time each year, and at no other. There is no conventional stage, curtains, scenery, wings or other paraphernalia of a theatrical venue, and, most important of all, the mummers *come to you*, not the other way round. Performances take place in everyday spaces such as kitchens, pubs, and streets. The performers are not professional actors; they are not even *amateurs* in the usual sense of the word as they do not usually take part in other dramatic activities.

Mumming performances appear to be based on a different set of principles to those of the theatre. However, it is probably the case that, over time, the performers themselves have gradually adopted a more theatrical attitude to the custom as they have become more self conscious and the context for the play has changed. Given the fact that most writers ignore style in their descriptions, and that comments which appear are often of a derogatory or ambiguous nature, the *manner* in which mummers performed in the past is probably the most difficult aspect of the custom to get to grips with.

A close reading of available sources, however, enables us to piece together what is probably a universal style for hero-combat mummers across the country.

*"They took the play very seriously ..."* and *"In their combats, as in the delivery of their lines, they appeared to be in deadly earnest"* are key phrases in a description by T.F. Ordish of mummers seen at Barnes (Surrey) in 1891. The picture that can be teased out of available descriptions is, basically, a serious demeanour, upright stance, minimal and stylised gestures, and much pacing up and down, especially when the combatants are challenging each other or clashing swords as they pass. Lines were delivered in an almost expressionless and loud declamatory style, without much attempt to represent character. This vocal style is particularly difficult for many commentators to cope with, and comments such as *"they didn't understand the words they were saying"* or *"lines delivered in a monotonous sing-song"* are common.

**The Mysteries of Mumming**: *There is an old custom still prevalent in the Western, and (I believe) Northern counties of this nation, which is, however, almost entirely unknown to the other parts of it. I allude to what is called `Mumming'. A few particulars on this subject may not be uninteresting; more especially, as the difficulty with which I abstracted them from the boys who perform in these mysteries, was by no means slight. To proceed to details. A number of youths - perhaps there may be seven or eight of them - having duly absented themselves from work for upwards of a week, make their appearance on Christmas-day, after divine service, clad in raiments composed of all the patch-work their unskilful hands can collect; - coloured paper and ribbands, begged from Miss at the Squire's; paints, stolen from the carpenter's; indigo, stolen from the old washer-woman, perhaps with the addition of what she denominates 'pink'; - all tend to set off the gorgeous dresses of the young mummers. Thus clad they proceed, first of all, to the Squire's house; where, if they can obtain a passage through the dogs, they are sure of meeting with friends and patrons among the gossips of the servants' hall. Master's permission is easily gained; and then one*

*of them opens...in a sort of indistinct murmur, between a growl
and a grunt, something of a monotonous sing-song; only broken
by the blows which he hits, with his wooden sword, against the
handle of his pike ...*

**[A.B., 'The Mysteries of Mumming',
The Crypt, Vol.2 (1828) pp.68-70]**

A degree of *ad lib* was admissible in some plays, but in the
overwhelming majority it was not. Generally, performers spoke the
lines as they had been taught - full stop! Further, some versions
appear to have been played as comedy. However, the majority of
plays were performed in a very serious, matter of fact manner. Even
the sword-fight, which provides the only real opportunity for *action*,
was normally underplayed.

There are, though, important exceptions to this rule of thumb. Firstly,
there is evidence in the south of England that the Father Christmas
character (usually the main Presenter) was played as a bent old
man, leaning on a stick (in stark contrast to the upright stance of the
others), with his lines being delivered with humorous overtones.
Secondly, the Doctor's speech would sometimes include humorous
lines, and his interplay with an assistant (e.g. Jack Finney or Molly)
provides scope for humour in their verbal by-play.

There is also evidence that performers behaved differently in differing
social settings. For example, the occasional 'broad' word or phrase
would be omitted when performing at the 'Big House' for their social
superiors, while pub audiences may have been considered to be
more understanding of the whole, unedited version. Certainly, the
prodigious amounts of alcohol known to have been consumed by
many adult mummers on certain occasions will certainly have
affected performances in one way or another. But there is little
evidence of performers attempting to encourage audience
participation, heckling, hissing, booing, and so on.

Where the space and shape of a performance area permitted, the
usual method of performance would be for the performers to stand
in a shallow semi-circle at the back, and 'entering' and 'exiting'
would merely be a matter of stepping forward or back into line. At

times, the mummers would assemble in a hall or corridor and use a convenient door through which to enter and exit, but this does not seem to have been thought necessary in most places.

There is considerable evidence of the performers bursting straight into a performance space and starting a play, rather than making some kind of formal announcement that it was about to begin. This was probably not practicable in many situations. For example, at big houses there would be codes of behaviour to observe and the need to gather children, guests and staff together for the show. It is more likely that the expected surprise visit could be carried out only within one's own community (where the recipients could be relied on to know 'the rules') and especially in pubs, which are public places anyway. Again, there is evidence that the surprise visit was increasingly discouraged from the late nineteenth century onwards.

Singing could also be part of the proceedings. Much of the Wooing/ Bridal / Recruiting Sergeant play was sung anyway, but some other texts have integral songs, or maybe sung verses at the end of a play. It was also common for the performers to entertain the company with songs (and/or tunes) after the completion of the play. Carols were the staple fare at Christmas time, but comic or sentimental songs are also commonly reported. The choice of song might vary with the audience.

**Surrey Mummers**: *The mummers, too, performed according to ancient tradition at various seasons. They consisted of young people, who were dressed in home-made fancy costumes, of divers shapes and colours, but invariably decorated by strips of paper, like those used for making the tail of a kite, sewn on to garments to imitate streamers. Each performer in his turn would step forward from his ranks into the range of a light from a lanthorn held by a comrade. He would announce his name and qualities in doggerel before joining in the dialogue. I believe the plays were very old and traditional, and the performers did not at all understand the meaning of what they were doing.*
**[Edgar Browne, *Phiz and Dickens* (London: James Nisbet, 1913) remembering Thornton Heath (Surrey) c1840s]**

*Hampshire Mummers with Father Christmas*

## Costumes

Another aspect of the mummers' performance which separates it from the formal theatre is costume. Where theatrical plays expect actors to dress in a costume which distinguishes and marks their character, until relatively recently most mummers dressed in such a way as to *all appear the same*. Over time, however, such uniformity has diminished. Photographic evidence and various descriptions show teams at various stages of development, with certain characters wearing distinct costumes some years before others. Characters with easily identifiable (and cheap to make) costumes - such as Father Christmas and the Doctor - were the first to succumb to the temptation to dress in part. Less easily defined characters, such as Twing Twang or Bold Roomer, often continued to be dressed in the older, anonymous style for many years afterwards.

It is often assumed that the mummers' costume is actually a *disguise*, designed to separate the performers from the everyday audience and to preserve anonymity (see, for example, Margaret Dean-Smith, 'Disguise in English Folk-Drama', *Folk Life* Vol.1 (1963) pp.97-101). There is little evidence for this, although other related traditions (such as the Mummering custom in Newfoundland) definitely include this element, and the question of disguise is therefore best left open at present. The idea is usually promoted as part of the pagan-origins/fertility-cult conception of the play and should be approached with caution. If the play really does stem from an eighteenth century source, then it is unlikely that disguise was a significant factor in the development of the costume. Support is perhaps given to the disguise theory by the name *Guising,* which is applied to the custom in various parts of the country, but this often meant simply 'dressing up'.

Dressing in character aside, mummers' costumes vary considerably from one place to another. The following basic characteristics can be identified:

**Streamers**: strips made out of wallpaper, rags or ribbons (or even newspapers, as at Marshfield) which are sewn onto everyday clothes and worn from head to foot.

**Fringes**: similar to streamers, but with the covering material trimmed into neater strips.

**Patches**: pieces of material, sometimes cut in a variety of geometric shapes or in the form of animals or other figures, which cover clothing; or sometimes in the form of rosettes.

**Everyday clothes**: the clothes you stand up in but sometimes with variations, such as turning coats inside-out.

**Hats**: these vary considerably, but are often extremely ornate and imposing. Decorated with wallpaper, tinsel or rosettes. Hats are often made of cardboard and about 18 inches (45cm) high. Sometimes fringes or streamers are suspended in front to completely obscure the face.

**Blackened faces**: in many versions, all over the country, performers blackened their faces with burnt cork or similar substance. This is also found in other traditional customs.

**Masks**: numerous early descriptions mention *masks*, but there is little evidence for their later use, apart from in children's performances, and the writers were probably referring to the face fringes suspended from the hats..

**Sword-Dancers**: some teams wear military-style uniform, while the accompanying 'characters' dress in character.

Props - or perhaps *equipment* is a better word here - were minimal. The combatants carried **swords**, which were usually made out of wood, although there are some references to metal ones. In some descriptions it seems that all the characters carried **sticks** or **staves**, possibly made from broomsticks, while Father Christmas invariably had a **walking stick** to lean on. The Doctor normally carried a **bottle** or **box of pills** - whichever was called for in his lines – and Beelzebub had a **frying pan** and/or **club**. Little Johnny Jack would often wear some **dolls** strapped to his back, and in some versions one of the presenters - especially the one who called for 'room' - carried a **besom**, with which they swept the floor as they spoke. An example here is the *quête* character Billy the Sweep, or Little Devil Doubt, in the pace-egg play.

Most teams would also have something to collect money in. This may have been a proper collecting box or quite simply a tambourine or hat which was passed around.

However, it should be noted that performers would often eschew most such equipment, even if the text called for them. The swords or similar weapons were probably the only absolute essentials.

> **A Gloucestershire Mumming Play**: *"If you please, the mummers have come". A shuffling of feet on stone flags, a hoarse base whispering, with a few strangled "hems" as of a nervous singer about to perform, show that a welcome has been taken for granted, and already the actors are in possession of their green-room, the long dark passage leading to the kitchen. The maids - town-bred and strange to such doings - half-frightened, half-giggling, stand peering into the dim shadows, where beings of more than mortal stature jostle one another. Each man grasps a long white wand (in ordinary life a broomstick, but a quarter-staff for the nonce), and on each head*

> *towers a huge fantastic head-dress covered with pieces of tinsel and bright-coloured rag, which gleam in the firelight as the wearer moves. The dresses are new this year. Instead of last year's streamers of rag and paper sewn on tunics of sacking, the mummers wear rudely fashioned coats and trousers of flowered chintz and gay flannelette - all but one; he always has a distinct and traditional costume of his own. The whole household is called together, the big kitchen table is pushed back, there is a momentary hush of expectation, and then out of the darkness into the ruddy glow steps one of the figures, and as the others join him you see that every face but two is blackened ...*
>
> **[The Times 3rd January, 1914, p.6; probably describing the play from South Cerney, Gloucestershire]**

# Venues

Venues varied from team to team, but most performed in a combination of the following:

- In the open, usually at pre-arranged places around a town.

- At the homes of relatively well-to-do residents in the area ("toffs' houses") or farmhouses. The play would sometimes be performed in the servants' hall for the family and the servants, often in the kitchen, but maybe in other rooms (providing their boots were not too muddy), or simply outside. The day and time of these visits was usually arranged well in advance.

- At public houses or where other social gatherings took place in the area.

- The homes of family, friends and neighbours, especially where the play was performed by children in urban areas.

- Town streets, where some accounts refer to teams 'busking' for passers-by (not a favourite when bad midwinter weather conditions were prevailing).

Travelling from venue to venue often involved covering large distances, and reports abound of teams walking over thirty miles a day in their rounds of a district. Later descriptions include travelling by horse and cart, by bicycle (not easy dressed in a mummers' costume!), on the back of a coal lorry, and even by bus.

*Marshfield Paper Boys, Marshfield, Gloucestershire*

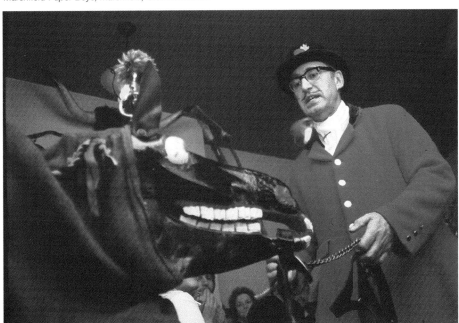

*Antrobus Soulcakers, Cheshire*

*Goathland Plough Stots, Goathland, North Yorkshire*

*Symondsbury Mummers, Dorset*

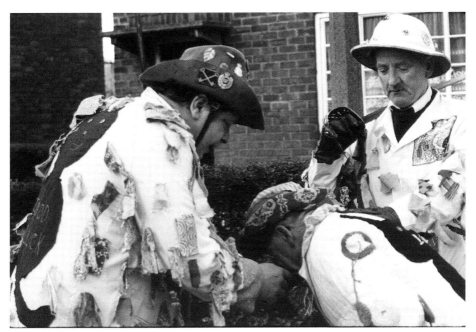

*Ripon Sword Dancers, Ripon, North Yorkshire*

*Limpsfield School Mummers, Sheffield, South Yorkshire*

*Abingdon School Mummers, Abingdon, Oxon.*

*Midgley Pace Egg Play. Calder Valley*

There is evidence that teams kept to regular territories, especially when there was another team nearby. There was certainly some rivalry between neighbouring teams, and mention of potential trouble if they met.

> **Wild Horse** - *It was customary until 30 or 40 years ago for the different gangs to come to blows and try to rob each other of their horses' heads; an amusing tale is told of the capture of one outside an inn at Whitley while the performance was actually going on inside, and of the surprise of the players when it was not there to come in and end the show.*
> **[A.W. Boyd, *A Country Parish: Great Budworth in the County of Chester* (London: Collins, 1951) pp.68-76]**

# Attitudes and motives

Very few of the available sources mention the participants' motives or attitudes towards the custom, and such evidence as we do have is drawn from interviews with latter-day mummers carried out in the last few decades. Every mummer to whom the authors have spoken stressed the economic aspects of mumming first. When asked why they did it, they detailed the amount of money they could make, what it was usually spent on (e.g. new shoes for the children), and the general poverty around at the time. Many also commented on the food and drink they consumed, although ironically such memories were not always pleasant. Sid Cole, one of Hampshire's North Waltham gang, said that over twenty years after giving up the mumming he still couldn't face a mince pie at Christmas!

Although clearly a functional activity for such men, it is also clear that a vital element in the perpetuation of mumming was the sense of camaraderie and shared experience that resulted from it. When asked if it was fun, the old mummers usually said that it was, but quickly qualified this by stressing how arduous it all was: the miles they had to walk, the nuisance it was to be away from their families over Christmas - "I never had a Christmas dinner [on Christmas Day] at home for over twenty-five years" (Sid Cole again) - and so on. After which they would recount the funny things that used to happen.

**An Easter Custom**: *Beyond the modernising sphere of industrial activity, many ancient and picturesque customs are clung to in rural districts, and among these is jollyboying, as it is observed in Westmorland...The writer's acquaintance with the custom is lifelong, for his whole life has been spent in the very locality [Bowston Bridge] in which it is observed. One of his earliest recollections is of being allowed to stay up and see a party act. It was a dark and windy night; the fitful gleams of a horn lantern illuminated the faces round the ring for a pulse, then threw into high relief the actors in their paper gewgaws and uncouth faces; then moved on to delineate the ivy-clad walls of the houses near. The memory is vivid, but an air of unreality seems to pervade it. Being a cottager's son, as the years rolled on he took a place in the cast, and went round acting. And what times and experiences they had! Visiting the outlying farmhouses just ere the farmers retired to rest, charging unceremoniously - maybe a relic of that privileged mummery of ancient days, of which the custom takes the place - into the low-ceiled, whitewashed kitchens, and acting without leave or consent. Occasionally the obtrusion was resented and the party hustled forth; but for years it had been tolerated, and now died hard. Now, however, we hear a knock on the door, and a timid voice asks, "Please may we act?". The sheep-dogs wherever we went used to harry us - figures with black faces and streamers of coloured paper came not within their philosophy - but the parties were not to be denied....Supper was always ready laid for us; lad-like, we rejoiced at the prospect of five or six suppers in one evening, without reproach from anxious parents, and for this we blessed Easter*

**[William T. Palmer, *Lake-Country Rambles*
(London: Chatto & Windus, 1902) pp.318-334]**

Underlying and occasionally explicit in these first hand comments was the sense that the mummers' play was an old custom and one of which we should be proud and continue to perform.

The recorded attitudes of performers' wives and families are even rarer, but they range from a dislike of the custom because the men drank away all the takings, to tolerance because it got them out of the way, and finally to pride because the mummers were something special and earned a few extra pounds in the process. However, blackened faces were particularly disliked by wives because of the toll they took on pillow-cases!

The attitudes of audiences also varied considerably. As already mentioned, some of the more well-to-do people whose houses were visited by the mummers, regarded it as the most pleasant and diverting interlude of the season, especially at Christmas time if they were entertaining guests from outside the area. Such people were often aware of the traditional aspects of mummers' performances and took a pride in helping to keep the old country customs alive. Children, however, were often scared stiff of these outlandish visitors

> **Twelfth Night Mummers**: *Twelfth night had come and gone, and life next morning seemed a trifle flat and purposeless. But yester-eve, and the mummers were here! They had come striding into the old kitchen, powdering the red brick floor with snow from their barbaric bedizenments; and stamping, and crossing, and declaiming, till all was whirl and riot and shout. Harold was frankly afraid; unabashed, he buried himself in the cook's ample bosom. Edward feigned a manly superiority to illusion, and greeted these awful apparitions familiarly, as Dick and Harry and Joe. As for me, I was too big to run, too rapt to resist the magic and surprise. Whence came these outlanders, breaking in on us with song and ordered masque and a terrible clashing of wooden swords?*
> **[Kenneth Grahame, *The Golden Age* (London: John Lane, 1898) pp.121-122; remembering his childhood at Cookham Dean, Berkshire, in the mid-1860s]**

Others, however, were presumably not so obliging. The attitudes of those who refused to accommodate the mummers are not generally recorded. However, it is now largely accepted that by the second half of the nineteenth century, many customary practices, and especially those which involved mass gatherings and alcohol, were seen as threatening to law and order. Hence, the middle class sought to control these activities as part of the attempt to impose a concept of 'rational recreation' on the leisure activities of the working class. The mummers, being a relatively small-scale and private affair, probably escaped much of the opprobrium at this time, but the propensity of mummers to drink a lot caused certain sections of the community to frown on them.

Another aspect of mumming which caused concern was its relationship to the stigma of begging. Previously, it had generally been accepted that participants in these customs could collect money - as long as they did so without threats - and *keep it for themselves*. Increasingly, however, those in a position to give money became more concerned with where it was going, and although collecting for charity continued to be acceptable, collecting for oneself inevitably became classed as begging. In areas where children kept the custom going, parents often vetoed participation because of the association. In more recent times, Penny-for-the-Guy and Carol Singing traditions have been beset with the same problems.

> **Spennymoor Guisers:** Before leaving the customs of the Whitworth pit lads it would be a pity to omit a reference to the 'Guisers', although guising or mumming is by no means peculiar to the locality, but still prevails in many parts of England. 'Guisers' are persons disguised, and the boys of Spennymoor conform to the ancient tradition by blackening their faces and wearing masks if they are able to afford them. It was formerly considered to be unlucky to refuse admission to the guisers, but they are now looked upon as more or less of a nuisance. Guising is fast dying out and it is now almost impossible to obtain an accurate version of the performance ...
> **[James J. Dodd, *The History of the Urban District of Spennymoor* (Spennymoor: The author, 1897) pp.117-121]**

A somewhat different complaint was directed at the Plough Jags, the performers of the East Midlands Wooing or Recruiting Sergeant plays. Here, the groups of men were much larger in number and the play was often accompanied by the dragging of a plough around the parish - a custom which also existed in its own right without the play. There are many stories of the threats - either implied or made

*Top: Plough Jags, Branston, Lincolnshire c1900*

*Left: Brant Broughton Plough Boys, Lincolnshire 1981*

explicit - against householders who refused to donate to the team, the least of which was to plough up their driveway or lawn. Passers by who refused to contribute could also be handled roughly. Local newspaper accounts of plough customs vacillate between 'quaint old English custom' and 'this outrage must stop' in direct proportion to the degree of threatening behaviour involved.

> **Lincolnshire Ploughboys**: *At Messingham they had a special display of hobby horses and it was the custom of the more venturesome to try to pluck their tails. If any stranger came he was almost certain to be asked to take a hand in this and would be greatly tempted by offers in pints of beer at the village pub to undertake what was apparently a very easy task. He found that, when once he got hold of the tail the difficulty was to let go again; for embedded in the hair were fish-hooks which invariably found their way deep into his fingers, amid roars of unfeeling laughter from those who had been watching ...*
>
> **['Northerner',** *Yorkshire Post* **12th January, 1937, p.6]**

*Ripon Sword Dancers, Ripon, North Yorkshire*

# Section 3    **A Guide** to Performance

## Getting **started**

Many schools now use the mumming play in one form or another as a class exercise. The introduction to this book has set out much of what is known about the origins of folk drama and the manner in which the mumming play was performed in the past. This should provide an adequate background for the presentation of a play in a school environment. It is a play which has an undoubted appeal to children, not least because of the sanction it gives to one or more sword fights. But before a sword is drawn in anger, some serious thought might first be given to the purpose for which plays were originally performed.

We have already indicated that the material rewards received (food, drink or money) were for many mummers an essential part of their reason for performing the play. Taking the pace-egging tradition in Lancashire as an example, Sim Schofield recalls that after their last performance of the day, he and his friends walked a distance of some five or six miles from Failsworth into Manchester to spend their money at the Easter Fair at Knott Mill. He also tells us that his share of the collection was 'one shilling and ninepence and three eggs,' a considerable sum for a young lad in the 1870s [S. Schofield, *Short Stories about Failsworth Folk*, (Blackpool: the author, 1905) p.12.] More recently, an inhabitant of Rochdale recorded that during the depression in the 1930s, he collected £2 at a time when his unemployed father received only thirty shillings a week (£1.50) 'means test' money to keep his family of seven. Recollections of this kind reinforce the concept of the play as a 'legitimised wealth transfer transaction' or begging custom, and also fix the play within the context of local history and tradition. They can often be found in the 'life story' booklets produced by oral and local history societies, or by adult education groups such as the Workers' Education Association.

In addition to these booklets (and of course the writings of nineteenth and early twentieth century antiquarians from which we have extracted many passages for this book), local newspapers are a valuable source of information on local play traditions. Many local history libraries have electronically indexed their newspaper collections for the benefit of researchers, and such databases will cover references to the local mumming plays. These libraries may also have collections of press cuttings and photographs covering a locality's traditions, which will also be indexed. All of these sources can be very revealing when trying to trace change within a tradition and changing attitudes towards it. For example, the columns of the *Rochdale Observer* for April, 1905, recorded the presence of the young pace-eggers in the following terms:

> *'... they continued to perambulate the streets until the late afternoon, adding much colour to an otherwise dull aspect, and providing considerable amusement in return for the coppers collected.'* [Rochdale Observer, 22 April, 1905]

By 1919, the paper's view was somewhat changed:

> *The "pace-eggers" were more numerous and, truth to tell, a greater nuisance than ever. We have nothing to say in depreciation of any good old custom, but this has degenerated into little more than an excuse for house to house begging by raucous voiced lads who are not content with their "dramatic" efforts on Good Friday morning, but are perambulating the streets for weeks beforehand. It is time it stopped. [Rochdale Observer, 19 April, 1919]*

Chapbooks are yet another source of printed information which, for example, help us to understand how young mummers in the past learnt their lines. Indeed, in some parts of the country play texts were produced in this form especially for children. Lancashire was rich in them and an illustration of their use can be found in J.T. Clegg's dialect sketch 'Bowd Slasher', which tells of a group of children performing a play in the streets of Rochdale. [J.T. Clegg, *The Works of John Trafford Clegg. Stories, Sketches, and Rhymes in the Rochdale Dialect,* (Rochdale: Clegg, 1895) Vol. 1, pp. 76-83.]

It is clear from the context that at least one of the boys has a copy of the local chapbook in his pocket. In 1895, on the other hand, Sim Schofield and his friends were taught their lines by a local handloom weaver, a fact which supports the view that many such workers were both literate and able to read books and chapbook texts whilst working. Again, local studies libraries, especially in the north of England, may have copies that can be consulted.

Information can also found within the family. Older members might have been mummers themselves and would have coached younger siblings in the text and performance of the plays. Alice Woodhead, who was born in 1878, recalled teaching the play to her brothers and their friends [Living History Workshop, *Do You Remember. Some Rochdale People Look Back to the Turn of the Century*, (Rochdale: Rochdale College of Adult Education, [1975]), p. 22]. Her story confirms the place that women often took in the passing on of traditions, even though they were not usually allowed to take part in them. Indeed, women are now widely recognised as the true tradition bearers within a community and it is worth asking around.

For a more detailed summary of information sources, see Section 4.

## Choosing **a text**

This book contains a number of texts of varying types, dates and places of origin, but we wish to emphasise that they are presented as examples only and do not have to be performed unchanged. The manner in which a text is used will, to some extent, depend upon the intention of the group performing the play. If the intention is to present a piece of local tradition at the appropriate time of the year, then such texts can be used unchanged (Section 4 suggests where additional play texts will be found if one relevant to you is not included in this book). However, if the intention is to use the *concept* of a mumming play as part of an English or drama project, then other approaches may be used and a non-local text may be more appropriate. For example, schools wishing to produce a play at Christmas may opt for a non-local text where the local play is an Easter custom (or, moreover, where none exist at all!). And vice

versa. Interestingly, Easter plays *can* be adapted for use at
Christmas and there is some evidence that in Lancashire they were.
The cast list appears to have been the same in both plays.

There are other reasons why changes or modifications might be
necessary. Sensitivity towards race and gender issues may dictate
that it is inappropriate to put on a play with characters such as the
Black Prince of Paradine and containing the lines 'you black
Morocco dog?' or 'Oh cruel Christian, what hast thi done?' It may be
considered more appropriate to rewrite or modify a play in these
circumstances. Such rewriting can be done by a class teacher, or,
as was the case at Banks Lane Junior School, Stockport, as a class
exercise, with the teacher (in this case Lisa Austin) providing the
core dialogue and the children encouraged to establish character
traits and the literary modes to be used in creating the new texts.
The children can then introduce their own lines, providing them with
a local identity that is closer to their everyday experience. Providing
that it is made quite clear to an audience that the finished play is
*based* on an earlier version of the mummers' play and not an
original, such re-writing can be a valuable learning process.

Similarly, it does not *have* to be assumed that the cast list is fixed in
size. Bury Girls' Grammar School produced a pace-egg play in
which there were parts for 23 children - a whole class. This was
achieved by having several clowns and 'Letters in', as well as using
some ingenuity throughout the play. One of the characters in the
play was Lord Collingwood, a sailor, and a regular in north
Lancashire versions of the play. When it was his turn to appear, he
came on with three of the crew of his ship. Such duplication of
characters does in fact have historical sanction. Alex Helm records
that, 'Often [mummers] were 'double gangs' with characters
duplicated, triplicated, and sometimes quadruplicated.' [A. Helm,
*The English Mummers Play*, (Woodbridge, Suffolk: D.S. Brewer,
1981), p.18.] These teams could split up and perform more plays
and increase the day's collection.

Another example of such ingenuity is from a teacher in Scotland
who successfully integrated a child with a bad stammer. A character
called 'Tea, Toast and Butter' was introduced into the cast and

when s/he came on it was with the lines, 'In comes I, t-t-t-tea, t-t-t-t-toast and b-b-b-butter'. The character was so popular that it remained a part of the play long after the afflicted child had left the school. Indeed, catering for enthusiastic children with special needs can be challenging, and where, for example, some boys and girls have difficulty in coping with a particular set of words or lines, it will be necessary to modify pieces of dialogue in order to make them easier to handle.

# Casting

Casting the play can be easy, especially if a small group of children exhibit particular keenness. However, certain principles should be borne in mind.

The 'Letter in' or Presenter should have a particularly loud voice in order to attract attention and establish the fact that something rather special is about to occur.

Combatants in the fight scenes should either be well matched or chosen deliberately to emphasise a disparity in size. In some Lancashire and Yorkshire pace-egg plays in which 'Bold Hector' is one of the combatants, he is played as a cowardly or 'wimpish' character. These traits can be emphasised if also played a large person.

The Doctor's part is usually the role in which most of the humour in a play is concentrated. Someone who can develop that humour should therefore play this character. If there is a class joker, this might prove to be the ideal part.

Beelzebub and Little Devil Doubt are two of the minor characters in many plays and can be foils for each other. Beelzebub is very effective if the part is played with some vigour. In some plays, he also comes on from a point completely different from that used by most of the other characters, thus introducing a degree of surprise into the performance. The aggression of Beelzebub can then be counterbalanced by Little Devil Doubt, whose part is usually played in a quieter manner.

Ultimately, of course, it is a question of using the human resources available. Even the shyest child might wish to take part, especially if s/he feels hidden within a costume. This attitude is frequently reflected by adult mummers who will do things in costume which they would not dream of doing in ordinary dress. Such is the power of disguise.

# Costumes

The first decision to be made is whether the actors will dress in role or in some non-representational costume. It is likely that most mummers in the past wore the latter type rather than a costume appropriate to the character. In Rochdale, for example, the mummers' dress was often a minimal change to their everyday wear. Actors blacked their faces, sometimes turned their coats inside out, and wore cloth sashes with rosettes stitched on them. Each character wore a different coloured sash. Up to the time of the First World War, these sashes could be purchased from the local newsagents, along with 'Strong Iron Swords' that were produced by Edwards & Bryning, who also printed the chapbooks from which the children often learned their lines.

By contrast, the children in Lancaster wrapped themselves in wallpaper, which was obtained from a local manufacturer. It is still possible to see performances in this type of costume in the South Cotswolds at Marshfield, Gloucestershire, where on Boxing Day the mummers act out their annual play. They are dressed in strips of newspaper' sewn to dairymen's coats or similar garments, hence their name the Marshfield Paper Boys. They also wear hats covered in similar strips and thus their faces are completely hidden from view.

The boys who act the Midgley Play in the Calder Valley also wear what is probably the vestige of a similar costume. Their dress consists of waist length smocks on which rosettes have been sewn. Most of the smocks are red but the Black Prince of Paradine, naturally, wears a black one. Smocks of this kind can be made

*Top: Sunningwell Mummers. Oxfordshire, 1936*

*Right: Marshfield Paper Boys, Marshfield, Gloucestershire*

*Abingdon School
Mummers, Oxon.*

relatively easily from old sheeting material. Using a piece wide enough and long enough to cover a child from shoulder to waist or thigh, this should be folded in half and a hole cut for the head at the middle of the fold. You now have a simple tabard which can be tied at the waist. You then need several pieces of colourful cloth which are about a foot (30cm) wide and as long as the tabard is wide. Cut this fabric into fringes and then sew several of them horizontally across the tabard at different points along its length.

Alternatively, an old shirt can be brought into service to act as the base garment. The paper ribbons used in Marshfield are difficult to sew, but the same, or a similar, effect can be obtained by sewing on ribbons of cloth.

The Doctor is traditionally dressed in a tailcoat and top hat or Bowler. These are hard to replicate but such items can sometimes be found in charity shops. An old dinner jacket may be more readily available than a tailcoat, or alternatively the doctor might be dressed as a hospital surgeon, with white coat and stethoscope.

Adult groups who act in costume often allow each actor to choose their own costume, depending on what they have available. Similarly, children can be encouraged to think creatively about their own costume, providing, of course, that the actor dresses within the conventions of the particular character. St George, for example, should always have a red cross about his person, either on a white tabard or on his shield, and preferably on both; while the exotic characters, such as the King of Egypt or the Turkish Knight, allow plenty of opportunities to use shiny, colourful fabrics for cloaks, tunics and pants.

# Props

The combatants will need **swords**. These can be made from 1½" (3.5cm) softwood, with the cross guards nailed or glued on, or simply tied on with string. If a basket guard is wanted, it can be made from thick card or thin plastic. Some imagination should be used in arming the knights. Amongst current mumming groups it is

probable to see fights with weapons in the shape of scimitars, halberds and battleaxes, in addition to the more conventional sword. All of these weapons can be made by children from softwood, hardboard and plywood, although this will depend to some extent on the resources available and/or the extent of adult help to hand.

Not all swords need to be of the same strength. The Lancaster

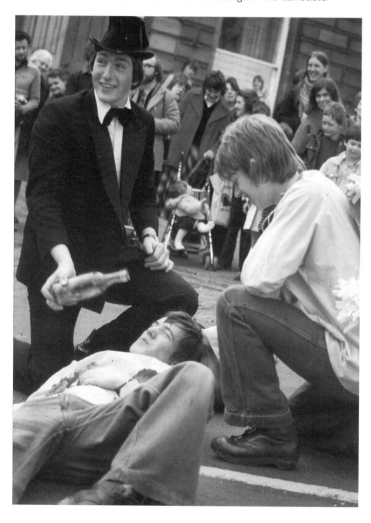

*Midgley Pace Egg Play. Calder Valley*

Pace-Eggers, for example, handicap St. George's enemies with swords made of flimsy orange boxwood, which breaks at the hero's first or second blow. Young children in the audience love this and come away with sword fragments as souvenirs. But however flimsy, mummers of any age can injure themselves during these fights and it would be prudent to ensure that all combatants wear thick gloves. After all, even real knights wore gauntlets!

Together with the swords, the combatants will of course need **shields**. These can be made from hardboard in a variety of shapes and then spray painted. The knights may also require some chainmail armour. This can be improvised by using silver spray paint on open weave dishcloths or onion and sprout sacks from greengrocers. Another alternative is the material which gardeners use to protect their soft fruits from the ravages of the local bird population. If the fabric is soft and porous, it may be necessary to soak it in size before applying the paint. When sprayed, these materials will be reasonably stiff - at least for the length of the performance.

**Crowns** can be made from cardboard, a Turkish **fez** from a plastic plant pot, and **helmets** from plastic basins. Metallic spray paints convey a remarkable degree of authenticity, but be careful when using it!

As suggested earlier, the 'healing' part of the play is often the source of most humour, although this is by no means an invariable rule. However, in plays in which the Doctor is to act the quack doctor or mountebank, his **medical bag** can contain a wide range of props ranging from a hammer ('It's anaesthetic, Mary'), to oil cans, saws, an alarm clock (with which to take the patient's pulse) and table tennis balls (boluses were large pills). A very common item for the Doctor's medical bag is a very large tooth, the extraction of which with anything from a large pair of pliers to a pair of coal-tongs, can be a rich source of humour. But ultimately, most cures rely on a bottle of some magic medicine, which in current plays ranges from whisky and Guinness to a token application from the mouth of any empty bottle. Whatever is chosen should enable the Doctor to milk his role for all the comedy you or the class thinks appropriate.

# Performance

It should be remembered that, in the past, mumming plays were mostly performed as a 'house visiting custom' and not as a public performance in an open space. In Lancashire, for example, there are records of teams visiting houses within the working-class community from which the actors came, additionally always making sure to knock on doors where the collection was likely to be more substantial than that which their immediate neighbours could provide. The households visited would therefore tend to be those of the wealthier members of local society: the factory owners and managers, the local doctor and other professional families, etc. In rural areas, this would mean visiting the large farms or the houses of the local middle-class residents. This is mainly the type of performance you will see replicated in some public houses today.

A major feature of these performances would have been the element of surprise when the mummers first appeared. Whilst they would not visit a house without being sure of a welcome, a conscious attempt at some semblance of surprise would be part of the visit. In a school environment, this feature of the play can be re-enacted if the play is presented to individual classes rather than to a whole school assembly. A proposed timetable of visits can be arranged with colleagues, leaving the audience to be surprised by the appearance of the mummers when the leader knocks at the classroom door. This mode of performance has been used successfully for the Christmas plays organised at Bank Lane Junior School.

If a performance is to be given in a school assembly, the audience is therefore not seeing the play in the manner in which it may have been originally intended. However, such a performance is closer to what most contemporary audiences understand by seeing a mumming play. And whilst performances in pubs do to some extent give the feel of a house visit, most mumming groups today also perform in streets and market places, even at folk festivals and such events as the Easter Maritime Festival at Lancaster. Audiences for these performances are similar to the audience for an assembly. So, do not be deterred.

*Sunningwell Mummers. Oxfordshire, 1936*

The place in which the play is to be performed will determine aspects of the style of the performance. If the performances are to be in the form of classroom visits then the characters can wait outside the classroom until they are called on to play their part. The Antrobus Soulcakers still perform their play in this way in the village pubs of Cheshire. If, however, the play is to be put on in an assembly, it will also be possible to perform in the way that earlier mummers did. Here the actors would come on to their 'stage' to whatever song or music is used; they would then stand in a semi-circle until it was time to play their part; the actor or actors would then step forward and perform before returning to the semi-circle or rank.

Whichever type of performance is used for the play, it is helpful to know that mummers in the past were rarely 'actors'. Hence, as the written records often indicate, they used to 'declaim' their lines rather than trying to modulate their voices as an actor would tend to do. School mummers, therefore, do not need to be trained actors, but merely have the ability to ensure that the audience can hear the words.

**Surrey Mummers:** *This evening, Jan 1 1883, a party of mummers performed outside my house in a remote part of Surrey, - half a dozen grown men, all wearing grotesque masks, strange hats, smocks or other guise over their clothes, all singing 'God rest ye, merry gentlemen' most mournfully, to the music of an old accordion. I did not comprehend those vagrom men, but gave them a coin - as who should say, "We may never see the likes of you again!"*
**[A.J.M. in *Notes & Queries 6th series, vol. 7* (1883) probably A.J. Munby of Wheeler's Farm, Pyrford, Surrey]**

Within any mumming play there are two principal points of action: the Doctor's healing ritual and the sword fight or fights. Whilst care is clearly necessary in arranging these scenes, they ought not to cause undue concern unless the knights see themselves as Errol Flynn, a Jedi warrior, or whoever is the contemporary equivalent. The text sets out who is to live or who is to die, or at least fall injured. The outcome is therefore clear and it is only a question of getting there with the minimum of difficulty. All that really need be conveyed to the audience is an understanding of the sequence of events. It is not necessary to convince them that they are witnessing a true battle between knights with all the verisimilitude that film and television has led us to expect. A few crossings of the swords are all that is necessary to indicate that a fight is taking place, before the death thrust under the arm achieves the objective. The same objective can be achieved if the actors strike swords during the 'boasting', which takes place before the fight. The principal thing is to convey a sense of the ritual rather than an exhibition of aggression.

# In **Conclusion**

Many schools have been successful in using traditional play material. Whether you choose to perform a play which was known in your area in earlier years, or whether you use a play text as the basis for a class exercise, I am sure that the children, at least, will enjoy the experience.

Having successfully produced a play at school, you might wish to consider taking it on tour. In the 1970s, some schools in the Rochdale area took their Easter play to nearby residential homes and pensioners clubs. In towns such as Rochdale, where there was a very strong tradition of pace-egging at Easter, older members of the community welcomed such reminders of past customs.

Many teachers who have successfully encouraged their classes to perform a mummers' play, were first stimulated by seeing a mumming team in action. Watching a performance by any of the present day mumming groups will help in an understanding of the nature of folk drama. It will also help to highlight the differences between one of these plays and a more conventional theatrical performance.

english**mummers**plays

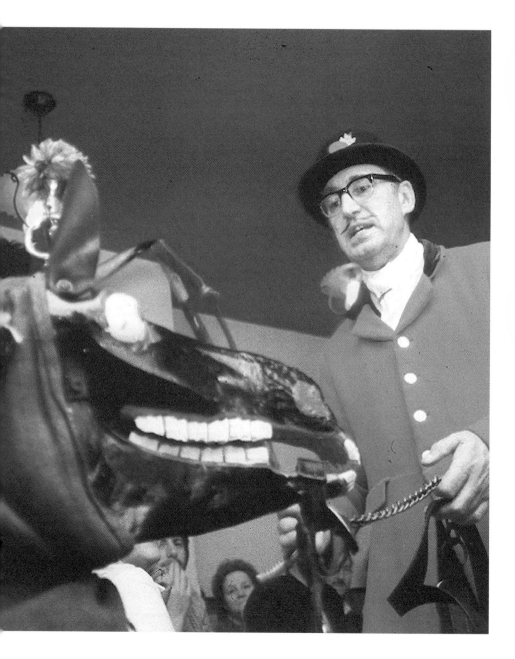

## Section 4 **Sources** of Information

# The English Mumming Play

*An introductory bibliography*

by Eddie Cass, Michael J. Preston and Paul Smith

'The English Mumming Play' available from the Vaughan Williams Memorial Library and The Folklore Society

The number of books and serious articles about the mumming play is limited. The best approach to these sources is **Eddie Cass, Michael J. Preston and Paul Smith, The English Mumming Play. An Introductory Bibliography (London: The Folklore Society, 2000)**.

In addition to these dedicated works, our information regarding mummers comes from a very wide range of sources, both primary and secondary. *Local newspapers* are a particularly fruitful source and can contain descriptions of contemporary performances, articles about their history, complete texts, 'notes and queries' sections about customs and antiquities, and so on.

Even *local court and police reports* can include references to fights, thefts, trespasses and the like carried out by mummers, while *obituaries* of well-known local characters can reveal a past mummer.

*National newspapers* and *magazines* will contain information from time to time, although this is often too generalised to be of much help. But *local history publications*, both academic and popular, often have a section on local customs and folklore which can include useful material. Published *autobiographies* might also include descriptions of mummers, usually from the point of view of the audience, but occasionally from the performer's side.

There is also a wealth of *unpublished material*, much of which is still in private hands. Collections of this type often include *photographs*, *manuscripts* of texts written down by performers, and *taped interviews* with ex-participants and eye-witnesses, which for 20th century mummers are our most important source of first-hand information.

*Left: Dick the Wild Horse and Driver, Antrobus Soulcakers, Cheshire*

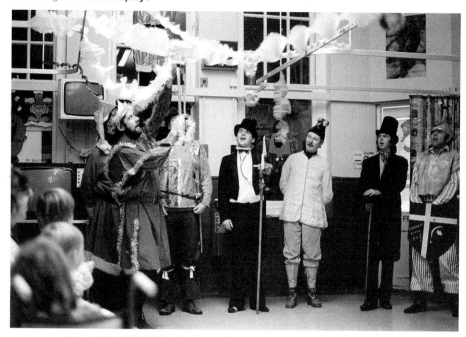

# Finding **material**

Given the limited number of dedicated sources available, plus the scattered nature and sheer quantity of others to sift through, only the persistent researcher can hope to gain access to anything but a handful of references to mummers within a locality. Indeed, it can be a daunting task for beginners to find anything at all! However, the publication of *English Ritual Drama* in 1967 provided information about 800 localities where mummers were known to have performed, and this could be your starting point. Listed by geographical location, many of the references included are to private collections and other sources, which may be difficult to find, but your local history library may hold some of the material mentioned. As *English Ritual Drama* (like most crucial works about mummers) is currently out of print, a trip to the local public library system might be on the cards in any case.

Since 1967, the number of references to mummers' and their plays has more than doubled, and new and old publications which include relevant information continue to turn up all the time. There is as yet no one institution which contains *all* the information known on the subject, although three institutions in England hold significant collections and will be able to help. These are:

**The Vaughan Williams Memorial Library**, English Folk Dance and Song Society, Cecil Sharp house, 2 Regent's Park Road, London NW1 7AY (Tel. 020 7485 2206) **www.efdss.org**

**The Folklore Society**, The Warburg Institute, Woburn Square, London WC1H 0AB (Tel. 020 7862 8562 or, with voice mail for messages, 020 7862 8564) **www.folklore-society.com**

**National Centre for English Cultural Tradition**, University of Sheffield, Sheffield S10 2TN (Tel. 0114 222 6296) **www.shef.ac.uk/english/natcect**

*Top: Rottingdean Tipteerers, Sussex*

*Left: Overton Mummers, Hampshire*

Each of these institutions can provide relevant information on request, but enquirers should note that none of them is adequately funded and do not have armies of staff waiting for your enquiry. To ensure success, plan ahead and be prepared to wait for an answer

- and be prepared to donate something towards the running of the institution over and above the cost of photocopies.

Additional help is also available from the following:

**The Morris Ring Archive Folk Play Section** seeks to hold copies of everything which has been written about the mumming play. Material can be consulted on application to the archivist, who will supply copies subject to copyright restrictions and required costs. The address is: The Morris Ring Archive, Folk Play Section, R.K. Shuttleworth, 41 Morningside, Coventry, CV5 6PD. (Tel. 024 7667 6721) **www.themorrisring.org**

The **Traditional Drama Research Group** maintains a web site which carries a number of play texts and has links to other important traditional drama pages. The address is **www.shef.ac.uk/uni/projects/tdrg.index.htm**

# Addendum

The performance notes have been written specifically with schools in mind. However, much of the information given can also be relevant to adult groups and any wishing to put on such plays on a regular basis are referred to R. Shuttleworth, *So You Want To Start Mumming? Suggestions for beginners* (Coventry: the author, 1985, repr. 1994). This work features aspects not covered here, such as group structure, affiliations and fees.

**Section 5**

# **Play** texts

## **1  Middle Rasen** (Lincolnshire) mumming play

From a 7-page typescript in the Opie Collection, The Folklore Society Archives. Reproduced by permission of Iona Opie and The Folklore Society.

The text was noted in 1953 by F.E. Fox of The Modern School, Market Rasen, from a recitation by Tom Sellars. It was sent to Iona Opie. A covering letter from the headmaster, S.B. Vickers, explains how the play was recorded:

*"Tom Sellars is quite a character, somewhere in his sixties I should say, and remembered going round the houses with this play when he was a young man, round Christmas times. He says he recorded this play for some visiting Americans a while ago"*

### **The Mummers or Morris Dancers**

List of characters, in order of appearance, with approximate details of dress:

**The Clown** - orthodox clown's dress, carrying a bladder on the end of a stick

**The Recruiting Sergeant** - dressed to suit the period, rather exaggerated

**The Lady** - ditto.

**St. George** - red sash round waist, hat rather like a crown, carrying sword, etc.

**Lame Jane** - sluttish and drab, using a sweeping brush as a crutch, carrying a doll (the "brat") under her free arm

**Beelzebub** - long grey beard and hump on back, large stomach,

dressed in an old shepherd's smock and a high hat

**The Doctor** - exaggerated version of a typical doctor, dressed in black coat, high wing collar and carrying black bag and stethoscope.

Also - **Concertina or Melodeon Player**

# The **play**

Enter *The Clown*

    Good evening ladies and gentlemen all.
This Merry Christmas makes me so bold as to call
I hope you'll not be offended at what I've got to say
For in a short time there'll be some lads and lasses this way
Some can dance and some can sing
And by your consent they'll now come in
Hokum, Sprokum, France and Spainy
In comes the Sergeant on the scene.

Enter *Recruiting Sergeant*

    In come I, the noble Sergeant
Arriving here just now
My order is to enlist all men
That follow horse, cart or plough
Likewise tinkers, tailors, peddlers, nailers
Any other fools at my advance
The more I hear the music play.
The better I can dance.

*Clown*    If thou begin to dance, sing or say.
I shall very soon march away.

Enter *Lady*    In comes a Lady bright and gay
Good Fortune and good smiles
Who mournfully was thrown away
Into some young man's arms.

*Clown*    Not at all, Madam
By the ring on your finger and the tear in your eye
Pray tell me what makes thee sob and sigh.

*Lady*    If you ask me to tell you the reason why
It's the thought of my young man that makes me sob and sigh
He swears if I won't marry him, as you shall understand
He'll list for a soldier and go to some foreign land.

*Sergeant* (sings) Come all you lads that's a mind for listin'

List and do not be afraid
You will have all kinds of liquor
Likewise kiss the pretty maids
Ten bright guineas shall be your bounty
If along with me you'll go
For your hats with ribbon shall be trimmed
Likewise cut a gallant show.

*Clown* (sings)    Now, kind sir, I'll take your offering
Time along will swiftly pass
Dash my wig, if I'll grieve no longer
For a proud and saucy lass.

*Lady* (sings)    It's true my love has listed and joined the volunteers
I never intend to wed with him nor even shed one tear
I never intend to wed with him, and I wish for you to know
For I have got another sweetheart and along with him I'll go.

*Clown*    Oh! You will have a waiting maid to wait at your command
If you'll consent to marry me, we'll be married off my hand.

*Lady*    My thoughts were of having a farmer's son

*Clown*    If they be your thoughts, Madam, I have done
Although my name is Rogers, I need not tarry long
Before I can get a wife
For there's old Boxing Joan, she's very willing
And she loves me as true as her life.

*Lame Jane* (calling from without)
D'ye mean me, me dear?

*Clown*    Ask my white leg, ye old bitch!

Enter *St. George*
In come I, St. George, with courage stout and bold
With my broad sword I've won ten thousand pound in gold
I fought the fiery dragon and brought him to the slaughter
By these few deeds I mean to marry the King's eldest daughter
I bashed him and smashed him as small as flies
And sent him to Jamaica to make mince pies.

*Sergeant*    Hold your lies, old man, or you will raise my blood
If thou be King, I dare face thee.

*George*    No King am I, 'tis plain to see

But with my broad sword I dare face thee
(*Then follows a small duel in the centre of the stage, with a considerable loud clashing of swords, etc.*)

Enter *Lame Jane (leaning on sweeping brush crutch, and carrying the "brat")*
In come I, old Lame Jane, paddling over the meadow
Once I was a bright young lady but now I'm a down old widow
Long I've sought thee, now I've caught thee
And since thou's called me a bad 'un
Tommy, take the bastard!
(*She hands the doll to the Clown, who looks at it, turns it over, and says*)

| | |
|---|---|
| *Clown* | Bastard, Jinny, why it's not a bit like me! |
| *Lame Jane* | Look at its eyes, nose, mouth, and chin<br>It's the picture o' thee, Tom, as ever it can grin |
| *Clown* | What is it, male or female? |
| *Lame Jane* | Female |
| *Clown* | Mine's all males - why thou 'ast niver seen me before in tha life, 'ast tha Jinny? |
| *Lame Jane* | Not as I knows on, Tommy! |
| *Clown* | Prithee, take the bastard, then! |

Enter *Beelzebub*
In come I, old Beelzebub
On my back I carry my club
Under my arm a whip-leather dripping pan
Don't you think I'm a jolly old man?
With my grey locks, they hang so low
I speak for myself as best I know.

| | |
|---|---|
| *Sergeant* | Wipe thy eyes, old man, and thou'll see clearer! |

*Beelzebub (pointing towards the stars up above)*
Methinks me sees a star shining bright
And in my heart it fixes a light.
(*The Sergeant strikes him across the stomach with his sword. Beelzebub falls to the ground face downward*).

*The Clown* calls out
Five pounds for the Doctor!

*The Doctor* (from without)
                Won't come under ten pounds!

*Clown*           Ten pounds for the Doctor!

(Enter the *Doctor*)
                In come I, the Doctor

*Clown*           How did you become a Doctor?

*Doctor*         Travelled for it!

*Clown*           Where did you travel?

*Doctor*         England, Ireland, Scotland and Wales
                Then back to old England doctoring again!

*Clown*           What can you cure?

*Doctor*         Ipsy, pipsy, palsy and gout
                If there's nineteen pains in, I can fetch one and twenty out!
                I have also limpins for grasshoppers, spectacles for blind
                mice,
                And I have a little drop o' stuff in a bottle here
                As will physic rats, poison cats, and bring dead men alive
                again

*Clown*           You seem very clever, Doctor!
                You'd better try your skill by feeling this man's pulse.
(The Doctor proceeds to put his hand on the top of Beelzebub's thigh!)

*Clown*           Is that where his pulse lies?

*Doctor*         Well, it's the strongest part about a working man, and beats
                the most regular!
                This man's been trying a new experiment.

*Clown*           What's that, Doctor?

*Doctor*         He's been trying to cut his throat with a rolling pin, and he's
                only in a trance
                Strike up the music and we'll all have a dance.

(Beelzebub jumps to his feet, and they take partners and dance a polka
round the room)
*George*         Stop! Stop! What's all this dancing and jigging about?

| Clown | Sport, father. My father was a great sportsman and a great jumper, too.<br>He once jumped so high he didn't come down for seven years. When he did come down, he had a wife and seven small children, of which I am<br>The oldest, the boldest, and the most terrible jumper of the lot! |
|---|---|
| George | Well, how did you come to be such a jumper? |
| Clown | I once jumped so high I dropped against a pretty milkmaid. |
| George | Did you court her? |
| Clown | Yes I courted her for the milk she sold<br>She courted me for the lies I told. |

*(Then the whole company join in and sing)*

Good Master and good Mistress, as you sit round your fire
Remember us poor plough boys that plough through mud and mire
The mire it is so very deep and the water is so clear
And we thank you for a Christmas Box and a drop of your good beer!

| Lame Jane | Aye, aye, and a bit o' your pork pie<br>I am as hungry as our old fool is dry! |
|---|---|
| Clown | Why you're always hungry, Jinny! |
| Lame Jane | Well, you're always dry, Tommy! |

*(She takes up her brush, and starts to sweep the floor)*

There's a little bit o' muck as I'll sweep up just here!

*(The Clown is first to leave the room, the rest all sing the closing chorus)*

Good Master and good Mistress, you see our fool has gone
We make it in our business to follow him along
We thank you for civility and what you've given us here
And we wish you Merry Christmas and a Happy New Year.

*(All troop out)*

# 2 **Chiddingfold** (Surrey) tip-teering play

From a 4-page typescript in the Vaughan Williams Memorial Library Collection. Sent to the Library by Margaret Balchin in April 1994. A covering letter explains that the text was dictated to her father-in-law (George Balchin, 1876-1956) by his father (c. late 1840s - mid-1920s), and typed from the original manuscript by herself.

### *"Tip-Teering" in Chiddingfold, Surrey, in 1860*
### *(Written by George Balchin, born 1876)*

*My Father told me that in his youth (the 1850's - 1860's), at Christmas time, he and other young men and lads of the village (Chiddingfold, Surrey) took part in the play-acting known as "tip-teering". They dressed for the parts as well as their restricted wardrobe resources permitted, and they blacked their faces with burnt cork. The combatant actors carried home-made wooden swords and the "Doctor" had his little bag of pills and potions.*

*There was evidently also some sort of puppet show for my Father spoke of "dolls dancing about" at the beginning of the play.*

*During the Christmas period the party visited all the larger houses and outlying farms in the parish. They were always welcomed and entertained, especially at the lonely farmhouses.*

*Ripon Sword Dancers, Ripon, North Yorkshire*

*Sussex Tipteerers*
*Courtesy Doc Rowe*
*collection*

*The spoken parts of the characters, and the order in which the latter appeared, as dictated by my Father, are given below. He had never seen a written or printed copy of the words: they had passed down by word of mouth and had presumably suffered some distortion. Thus St. George has become "King George".*

*It is possible that in my Father's recital one or two characters may have been omitted. He quoted from memory, and he was over 80 years at the time.*

| | |
|---|---|
| **Father Christmas** | **Turkish Knight** |
| **Little Billy Wittell** | **Gallant Soldier (Slasher)** |
| **Noble Captain** | **Noble Doctor** |
| **King George** | **Beelzebub** |

# The **play**

*Father Xmas*
In comes I, Old Father Christmas
Welcome or welcome not
Sometimes cold and sometimes not very hot
I hope old Father Christmas will never be forgot

*Little Billy Wittell*
In comes I, little Billy Wittell
Ladies and gentlemen I think this room quite little
Place by* these tables and chairs and stool
For after me comes men so cruel.

(* put aside, i.e. make room)

*Noble Captain*
Room, room, ladies and gentlemen
Room I pray
For I am a noble captain
That leads King George and his men this way.

*King George*
In comes I King George
That man of courage bold
With my broad sword and spear
I fought through many tons of gore
I fought a fiery dragon
And brought him to the slaughter
Therefore I shall win the Queen of Egypt's daughter.

*Turkish Knight*
In comes I the Turkish Knight
Comes from the Turkish land to fight
I'll fight King George with his courage bold
And if his blood's hot I'll soon make it cold.

| George | Hold, hold, you Turkish dog |
|---|---|
| | Do not so rip on |
| | For if you do I shall cut you down |
| | With my old trusty weapon |
| | I'll rag you and gag you for to let you know |
| | That I am King George of old England O. |

| Gallant Soldier | In comes I a gallant soldier |
|---|---|
| | Slasher is my name |
| | Sword and buckler by my side |
| | For to win the game |
| | Me and seven more fought and killed seven score |
| | March in, men of war |
| | Many such battles I have been in |
| | For to save George our King |
| | And for that King George shall have his will |
| | This Turkish dog I will soon kill. |

| Turk | Oh will you |
|---|---|

*(They fight with wooden swords and soon the Turk falls dead)*

| George. | Oh fie, oh fie, this man is slain |
|---|---|
| | And on the floor his body lain |
| | Is there a Doctor to be found |
| | To raise this Turk up from the ground? |

*(Doctor comes forward)*

| Noble Doctor | Oh yes, here is a noble Doctor |
|---|---|
| | And that you can plainly see |
| | Many years have I been a Doctor |
| | Both on land and on the sea |
| | And I am here before your Majesty. |

| George | Pray Doctor try your skill |
|---|---|

| Doctor | Try my skill? - fetch my horse Jack and I'll be gone |
|---|---|

| George | Pray Doctor, what is your fee? |
|---|---|

| Doctor | Fifty guineas is my fee |
|---|---|
| | And half the money I demand from thee |

| George | Oh dear, Doctor that can never be |
|---|---|
| | That is far too much for me |

| Doctor | Fetch my horse Jack, and I'll be gone |
|---|---|

| George | If fifty guineas is your fee<br>Half the money I'll give to thee |
|---|---|

| Doctor | Now King George you speak like a man<br>Now ladies and gentlemen you see I am not<br>One of those quack Doctors that goes about<br>From house to house and from door to door<br>Telling you as many lies in one half hour<br>As you will find true in seven years<br>What I do, I do before your face<br>And if you can't believe your own eyes<br>It must be a very bad case. |
|---|---|

*(Doctor sets to work, produces a box of pills which he calls "quick risers" also a bottle of "Snip-snaps", a drop or two of which, together with a pill, he places in the mouth of the fallen Turk. He moves the body about and after a time the Turk moves).*

| Doctor | He begins to breathe already |
|---|---|

*(They raise him up halfway, and finally upright)*

| Doctor | Rise, rise, dead man and walk<br>And see how nicely you can walk<br>Behold the cure that I have done<br>I have raised this Turk up from the ground<br>Now King George you see what 'tis to be slain<br>And to have a noble Doctor to raise the dead to life again. |
|---|---|

| Beelzebub | In comes I little Beelzebub<br>On my shoulder I have a knob<br>In my hand I carry a can<br>And don't you think I'm a funny little man?<br>Now ladies and gentlemen put your hands in your pockets<br>And make your money ring<br>And we will all sing. |
|---|---|

*(Goes round with his can. Others sing)*

# 3  **Coxwold** (Yorkshire)
## Blue stots/Plough stots

James Madison Carpenter was an American academic visiting Britain in
the 1930s ostensibly to collect ballads. This is a 2-page typescript with
manuscript additions from the James Madison Carpenter Collection,
courtesy of the Library of Congress.

### **The Blue Stots**, Coxwold

*"[Text from] Mr. A.J. Fox, Coxwold, York — learned fifty years ago —
from the older players — older brothers. Never saw in print. Been
played for generations. Played at First Monday in New Year, called
"Blue Monday". Sword dancers Christmas week.
Belzebub had blacked face and coat turned wrong side out; King
George dressed as a soldier; with sword and red coat, artificial black
beard; Brave soldier dressed as soldier. Different colored ribbonds
stitched to clothing. King George had round hat — combatants
fought with metal swords — went a week or two. Mr. Fox went
several years, up to thirty years old; began as a lad ten years old —
Belzebub never knocked: always banged door with club, and bolted
right in. Sometimes frightened bairns nearly out of wits. Sometimes
host waited until players had got nearly half way through piece, then
up with a stick, and make for them. Then came a scramble to get
out of door."*

| | |
|---|---|
| **Belzebub** | **Brave Soldier (Bold Slasher)** |
| **King George** | **Doctor** |

## The **play**

| | |
|---|---|
| *Belzebub* | In comes I old Belzebub |
| | On my shoulder I carry me club |
| | In me hand a frying pan |
| | I think meself a jolly old man |
| | A jolly old man I ought to be |
| | I have three sons as jolly as me |
| | If you won't believe one word I say |
| | Step in, King George, and clear the way. |
| | |
| *King George* | I am King George the valiant man |
| | Who spilt his blood all over England, Ireland, Scotland and Wales |
| | If you won't believe one word I say |
| | Step in, Brave Soldier, and clear the way. |
| | |
| *Brave Soldier* | I am Brave Soldier |

Bold Slasher is my name
Broadside and buckle, sir
I'll meet you in the game.

George    Meet me in the game sir
I don't think you are able
My back is made of iron
My belly's made of steel
My hands is made of knuckle bone
And that I'll let you feel.

*(King George knocks down with sword)*
George    There's poor Brave Soldier laid down on the floor
Send for a doctor

*Doctor* (comes in)
I'm the doctor

George    What's your name?

Doctor    E-vo, I-vo Ick-Tick Ten

George    Where do you come from?

Doctor    Itty Titty, where there's neither land nor city
Black puddins for bell ropes
Wooden churches, leather bells
Little pigs runnin' up and down the streets
Singing 'God Save the King!'

George    What's this man's ailments?

*Doctor* (examines) His back's out of creak (cree-uk)
Knees up back; Tick-tell-er-oo in his big toes
I've got a little bottle here called, Eurum-cum-curum
If he gets a little bit in his sniff-snaff, and chiff-chaff
Rise up, Jack, and fight again!
(Soldier gets up)

[All sing]
Four jolly fellows all in one row
If you give us aut, we'll take aut        [aut = owt = anything]
If you give us naut we'll take naut      [naut = nowt = nothing]
If you don't believe one word I say
If you give us naut, we'll take naut

## Commentary

An example of the short Hero-Combat play which has little but the bare essentials. Such texts are quite common in the Northern counties of England, especially where children kept the custom alive. Compare this text with the one from Sedgefield, Co. Durham. The title 'Blue Stots' is a reflection of the local pronunciation of 'Plough (Ploo) Stots'. Another text for Coxwold, collected within a few years of Carpenter's, was published by Douglas Kennedy in the *Journal of English Folk Dance Society* (2nd series Vol.3 (1930) p.38.). Kennedy heads his text:

> *The play was performed just a few days before Christmas. The Valiant Soldier wore a red sash crosswise over his shoulder and the Doctor had a top hat. There was another character, now dropped out, and called the Bride, who wore a lace curtain as a veil. If this comment about 'The Bride' is true, it would, as far as I know, be a feature unique to this version.*

Apart from a number of minor verbal differences, Kennedy includes a few lines missing from the Carpenter text, and vice versa. The Kennedy extras are mostly confirmed by a third description published about the same time, which gives some lines of the text only (The Northerner, 'Another Plough Stot Version', *Yorkshire Post* 15 Jan, 1937, p.8). Most notably, in the dialogue with the Doctor, Kennedy gives:

| | |
|---|---|
| *George* | *Where do you come from?* |
| *Doctor* | *Itty-titty, where there's neither wall nor city* |
| | *And little pigs run about singing 'God Save the king'* |
| *George* | *What's your fee?* |
| *Doctor* | *Eleven pounds, eleven shillings, and eleven-pence* |
| | *three farthings* (He |

kneels down and examines the dead man)

> *Broken jaw-bone with eating fat bacon*
> *Cramp in his belly*
> *And tic-taleroo in his big toe-nail*
> *I've a little bottle here called Im-cum-curum*
> *Take one sniff-snaff-jiff-jaff*
> *Rise up and walk.*

(The dead man rises).

The three sources do not necessarily agree on dates. Carpenter's informant learnt it about 1884 and performed up to about 1904. The *Yorkshire Post* says it was performed up the First World War and a subsequent attempt at revival failed. Kennedy is ambiguous, as he says *'was performed'*, but *'now dropped out'*.

# 4 The Sowerby Sword Play (Yorkshire)

Sowerby is on the outskirts of Thirsk, North Yorkshire. In the play are six dancers, three Clowns, and two musicians - a fiddler and a drummer. The dancers wore high hats without ribbons, pink jackets covered with rosettes and bows of ribbon, "as many as each could put on," and white trousers. One of the Clowns was dressed as a woman in a crinoline dress.

The music for the dance was usually done to the tune 'The Girl I Left Behind Me' or 'Down Falls the Palace'. There are also three songs during the performance.

For full details of how this dance is performed, see *'Longsword Dances from Traditional and Manuscript Sources'* by Ivor Allsop *(1996)*

## The **play**

*The play begins by one of the dancers speaking the following:*
>Make room, make room, brave boys,
>And give us room to sport,
>For in this place we mean to exalt.
>Exalt, exalt and show you many (or merry) rhymes
>Gentlemen and ladies it is Christmas time.
>Christmas comes but once a year
>When it comes it brings good cheer.
>Roast beef, boiled beef,
>Yule cake and apple pie,
>But very small share for you and I

*The dancers all sing the* Calling-on Song

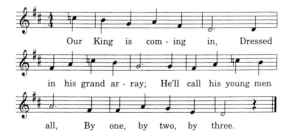

>Our King is coming in,
>Dressed in his grand array;
>He'll call his young men all,
>By one, by two, by three.

*The King then enters and sings to the same tune. The dancers follow the King round in a circle as they are called on.*

King.

The first that I call on,
His name is King Tom;
He has got lovers three,
But swears he'll marry none.

King Tom.

If I should marry one,
The others would me slight,
So it's best to marry none
And make them all alike.

King

The next that I call on,
He is a Squire's son;
He nearly lost his love
Because he was too young.

Squire's Son

Although I am too young I've money for to rove
I'll freely spend it all before I lose my love.

King

The next that I call on,
He is a tailor bold;
Stitches for woman's kind
And serves both young and old.

Tailor

Now with my goose I press,
The clothes I've fashioned well;
And mark you all the dress
Makes man look quite a swell.

King

The next that I call on,
It is bold Robin Hood;
He makes his arrows fly,
In merry old Sherwood.

Robin Hood

Bold Robin Hood am I,
Along with Little John;
We'll make our foes to fly,
If they be ten to one.

King

The next that I call on,
He is a sailor true;
With Nelson at Trafalgar,
He did his duty do.

Sailor

I mean to act my part,
Though we be called to war;

*Goathland Plough Stots, 1950 Photo: Yorkshire Post. Courtesy Doc Rowe collection*

I will my duty do,
A jolly English tar.

King         The last that I call on
A gentleman's son he was born;
For bacon and beef just look at his teeth,
He's a laddie for picking a bone.

All         We are six Sowerby lads,
As blythe as you may see;
We dance you a sword dance
To please the company.

*(All sing together)*
You've seen us all go round,
Think of us what you will;
Music strike up and play,
'The Lass of Richmond Hill'

*(All dance)*

*The King then sings* [Tune No. 2]

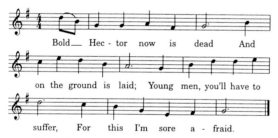

Bold Hector now is dead
And on the ground is laid;
Young men, you'll have to suffer,
For this I'm sore afraid.

Dancer       Don't lay the blame on me
I am clear of the facts
I am sure my eyes were shut
When this young man did fall.

King         How could your eyes be shut
When you were looking on
When you were looking on
When this false deed was done.

Dancer       Since you've laid the blame on me

|  | You villains all at last |
|  | Down on my bended knee |
|  | The pardon I will ask. |

| *A Clown* | Arise young man |
|  | And a pardon you shall have |
|  | Is there never a doctor in this place |
|  | This young man's life can save? |

| *King* | A doctor, a doctor to be found! |
|  | I'll give £5 for a doctor. |
|  | If there's never a doctor I'll give £10. |

*The Doctor enters with a small bottle in his hand saying:*

| *Doctor* | I'm a doctor right and good |
|  | And with my sword I've lanced blood. |

| *King* | How came thou to be a doctor? |

| *Doctor.* | By my travels. |

| *King* | How far have you travelled? |

| *Doctor* | I have travelled from Kitti-kitti |
|  | Where there's neither land, house or city |
|  | And I have travelled England, Ireland, |
|  | Scotland and Wales, High Low Germany |
|  | Africa, Asia, America, France and Spain |
|  | And now I'll return to cure this young man |
|  | With his nose on the stane. (stone) |

| *King* | Well! doctor, what is thy fee? |

| *Doctor* | Ten pounds, |

| *King.* | Pooh! pooh! That is sadly too much doctor! |

| *Doctor.* | Well it's only loosing my labour and coming and going back again. |

| *King* | Well, doctor, I'll see thee paid or unpaid in the morning. |

| *Doctor* | Well a bird in the hand is worth two in the bush. |

| *King* | Well doctor can you cure that young man? |

| *Doctor* | Yes. |

*(feels him all over, produces his bottle and holds it under his nose)*
　　　　　　Arise! Arise!

*Clown. (getting up) sings:*
　　　　　　Good morning Gentlemen,
　　　　　　A-sleeping I have been
　　　　　　I have had such a sleep,
　　　　　　As the like was never seen
　　　　　　A-sleeping I have been,
　　　　　　But now I am awake
　　　　　　So now I must away,
　　　　　　And see the doctor paid.

*All. sing to tune no 3)*
　　　　　　Then it's gentry and sentry all stand in a row
　　　　　　I wish you no manner of ill
　　　　　　I wish you all sweethearts that you and me court
　　　　　　So ladies we bid you farewell.

# 5 Sedgefield (Co. Durham) Guysers

James Madison Carpenter was an American academic visiting Britain in the 1930s ostensibly to collect ballads. During his visit he also recorded many mumming plays and the Sedgefield play is an example of a Guysers' Play.

This is Carpenter's description of the performance as found in his two-page typescript in the James Madison Carpenter Collection, Library of Congress, collected in the 1930s. By kind permission of Library of Congress. (Some spelling corrections have been made to the printed text here.)

### The Guysers, Sedgefield
"Mr. Thomas Thompson—Mr. Joseph Smith—Learned forty years ago—from older players – never saw in print—blacked faces, Colored suits, swallowtails, - blacked faces—rosettes tall hats—shiners—Dr. Brown with frock coat—fought with wooden swords—run through a belt"
Also in hand-writing above the text is "Dictated by three men - poor, of no account"

| | |
|---|---|
| First Man | King George |
| Third Actor | Doctor |
| Johnny Funny | |

## The play

**First Man**
I open the door, I enter in
I hope the game will soon begin
Stir up the fire and make a light
For in this house there'll be a fight
If you don't believe the words I say
Step in King George, and clear the way.

**King George**
In comes I, King George
King George is my name
Sword and pistol by my side
I hope to win the game.

**Third Actor**
The game, Sir! The game, Sir!
It's not within your power
I'll cut you up in inches
In less than half an hour

**George**
You, Sir!

**Third**
I, Sir!

| | |
|---|---|
| *George* | Take your sword and try, Sir! |
| *(They fence with wooden swords; Third Man goes down)* | |

| | |
|---|---|
| *George* | Horrible, horrible, what have I done |
| | I've killed my father's eldest son |
| | Call the doctor! |

| | |
|---|---|
| *Doctor* | In comes I, Doctor Brown |
| | The best old doctor in the town. |

| | |
|---|---|
| *George* | How comes you to be a doctor? |

| | |
|---|---|
| *Dr.* | By my travels |

| | |
|---|---|
| *George* | How far have you travelled? |

| | |
|---|---|
| *Dr.* | From the bedstock to the fireside. |

| | |
|---|---|
| *George* | Is that all of it? |

| | |
|---|---|
| *Dr.* | Naw, not half of it. |
| | I've travelled from Ittally, Pittally, Germany and Spain |
| | And now I've come to cure old England again |
| | Here, Jack, take a drop of my nip-nap |
| | And let it run down thy chip-chapp |
| | Rise up, and fight again. |
| *(Gives him a drink and he rises again).* | |

| | |
|---|---|
| *George* | Me brother's come to life again |
| | We'll never fight no more |
| | We'll be as kind as brothers again |
| | As ever we were before. |

| | |
|---|---|
| *Johnny Funny* | Here comes Johnny Funny |
| | That comes in to gather the money |
| | Holes in me pockets, holes in me cap |
| | But we have an old tin can |
| | To carry the cash. |

## Commentary

A second example of a standard short text from the North of England.
Compare with the play from Coxwold (number 3).

*Top and left:
Christmas Play,
Hampshire. Courtesy
Doc Rowe
collection*

# 6 **Bury Pace-Egging** play

The Bury Pace-Eggers were founded in 1970 and perform their play each Easter in Bury and many of the surrounding villages. The text of the play was taken from the autobiography of J. Barlow Brooks, a Radcliff mill lad who later became a Methodist minister [J. Barlow Brooks, *Lancashire Bred*, Headington: the author, nd. (1949)]. The text is unusual in that there is only one fight in the performance, which may represent the local tradition but could equally be a failure of recollection on the part of Brooks. This version is transcribed from a recording in the possession of the authors, with the permission of the Bury team.

The costumes now worn by the actors are influenced by conventions which emerged from the post Second World War folk revival. On entering, St George carries a metre-long model of a dragon.

## The **play**

*All enter, singing.*

> Here's one, two three jolly lads all in one mind
> We've come a pace-egging and I hope you'll prove kind
> An' I hope you'll prove kind, with your eggs and strong beer
> And we'll come no more nigh you until the next year.
> Fol-de-dee, fol-de-di, fol-de-diddle-di-dom-day.

*Fool (entering)*

> I open th' door. I enter in.
> I 'ope yer favour we shall win.
> Stir up th' fire an' strike a leet.
> Now watch mi merry lads act to-neet.
> Whether we stand or whether we fall,
> We'll do our best to please yo' all.
>
> So, room! room! brave fellies all
> Pray give us room to rhyme.
> We've come to show you visions
> This 'appy Easter time.
> An' if yo' don't believe what I say:
> Step in Saint George and clear the way.

*St. George (enters)*

> In come I, mon o'courage bowd.
> Wi' mi broad axe an' sword
> I won a crown o' gowd.
> I fowt this feighery dragon
> An' drove 'im to th' slaughter.

*(throws the dragon over his shoulder)*

> An' bi these means aw won
> Th' king o' Egypt's daughter.

> Show me th' mon 'at bids me stand,
> An' I'll cut 'im down wi' mi reet 'and.

*Bold Slasher (enters)*
> In comes I, th' Turkish Knight.
> Come fro' Turkish land to feight,
> Come to feight Saint George;
> This mon o' courage bowd.
> An' if 'is blood runs 'ot
> I'll soon turn it cowd.

*St. George (steps forward)*
> Stand back, Slasher, an' let no more be said
> Fer if I draw mi sword I'll surely break thi' yed.
> Thah speakest bowd to such a mon as me;
> I'll cut thi i' smo' pieces , an' bend thee at thi knee.

*Slasher*
> 'Ow conti break mi yed? Mi yed is made o' iron;
> Mi body's made o' steel, mi 'ands an feet is knuckle bone.
> No man con make me kneel.

*St. George*
> Then draw thi sword an' feight; er draw thi purse an' pay.
> Fer life er payment aw mun 'ave before aw end this day.

*Slasher*
> No life er payment shalt theh 'ave
> Fer wi' this sword thi yed aw'll cleave.

*St. George*
> Then guard thi body an' mind thi yed,
> Or else mi sword shall strike thi dead.

*Slasher*
> One shall live an' t'other shall dee;
> This is th' challenge I'll give thee.

*(They fight, and Slasher falls)*

*Fool*
> O cruel Christian! What hast thi done;
> Toho's wounded and slain mi only son.

*St. George*
> He challenged me to a deadly feight,
> An' never shall Saint George deny it.

*Fool (calling out to the crowd)*
> O! is there a doctor to be found
> To cure this deep and deadly wound?
> Doctor! Docter! Where art thee;
> Mi son is wounded to the knee!
> Docter! Docter! Play thi part;
> Mi son is wounded to the heart.

|  | I'll put down a thousan' pound |
|---|---|
|  | If e'er a Docter could be found! |

| Doctor | Aye! there's a docter to be found |
|---|---|
|  | To cure 'is deep and deadly wound. |
|  | I'm a docter, pure and good, |
|  | An' wi' my right hand I'll staunch 'is blood. |

| Fool | O! where ast'ee bin, an' fro' wheer 'ast 'ee come? |
|---|---|

| Doctor | Italy, Sicily, Germany, France an' Spain: |
|---|---|
|  | Three times round th' world an' back agen. |

| Fool | What cant' ee do, an what cant' ee cure? |
|---|---|

| Doctor | O soarts o' diseases; |
|---|---|
|  | Just what mi physic pleases |
|  | Th' itch, th' stitch, th' palsy an' gout; |
|  | Rheumatics inside and pains without, |
|  | If th' devil's inside I'll drive the bugger out. |
|  | I've got a little bottle bi mi side; |
|  | Its fame 'as travelled far an' wide; |
|  | Th' stuff i' theer's Elecampane: |
|  | It'll bring poor Slasher to life agen. |

*(the doctor approaches Slasher)*

|  | A drop on 'is yed, a drop on 'is 'eart, |
|---|---|
|  | Get up bowd felly an take' thi part. |

*(Cheers as Slasher rises again)*

| Bighead | In comes I, as 'asn't bin in yet |
|---|---|
|  | Wi' mi big yed an' little wit. |
|  | Mi yed's so big an' mi wit so smo' |
|  | I'll dance a jig an please yo' all. |

*(He dances to the sound of the melodeon)*

| Beelzebub | In comes I, Beelzebub. |
|---|---|
|  | O'er mi shoulder aw carry a club. |
|  | In mi 'ond a drippin pon. |
|  | Don't yo think aw'm a jolly owd mon? |

*(Loud 'No' from the audience)*

Johnny Jack *(enters with two or three stuffed figures on his back)*

|  | In comes I, little Johnny Jack. |
|---|---|
|  | An, two or three young uns at mi back. |
|  | It's yer money we want, of yer goodness crave, |
|  | Then we'll sing a song an' tak our leave. |

| *(All sing)* | Owd tosspot, owd tosspot, owd tosspot you see |
|---|---|
|  | Wi a bunch of blue ribbons tied down to his knee |

He's a wary owd man, an he wears a pigtail
And he's always delighted in drinking old ale.
Fal-a-day, fal-a-day, fal-a-diddle-l-dun-day.

Jack the sailor kilt his wife
Cut her up with a carving knife.
Weep away, weep away
Play the fiddle we're all so gay,
We're all so gay, we're all so gay,
Play the fiddle we're all so gay.

Down in Bent's meadows ther's plenty of bugs
They jump in your pockets and out of your lugs.
We'll get a sharp knife and cut their yeds off
An we'll have a good supper of bugs yeds and broth.
Fal-a-day, fal-a-day, fal-a-diddle-l-dun-day.

First that does step in, is our noble Fool
An' lads if you believe me, he's never bin to school.
Right falera-laddy, right falera-laddy.

Next that does step in, is our noble George
An' lads if you believe me, he wears 'is mother's draws.
Right falera-laddy, right falera-laddy.

Next that does step in, is our noble Slasher
An' lads if you believe me, he makes a good egg smasher.
Right falera-laddy, right falera-laddy.

Next that does step in, is our Doctor Quack
An' lads if you believe me, he cured poor Slasher's back.
Right falera-laddy, right falera-laddy.

Next that does step in, is our Beelzebub
An' lads if you believe me, he's ne'er seen t' washing tub.
Right falera-laddy, right falera-laddy.

Next that does step in, is our Bighead gay
An' lads if you believe me, we're all goin' away.
Right falera-laddy, right falera-laddy.

Next that does step in, is our Johnny Jack
An' lads if you believe me, next year we're coming back.
Right falera-laddy, right falera-laddy.

*Fool*   Ladies and gentlemen, our play is ended
Our money box is recommended.
Five or six shillings won't do us any harm
Gold and silver if you can.
Thank you.

# 7 **Chapbook** text

During the late nineteenth century, mumming play texts were circulated in north-west England by means of chapbooks - 8 page booklets printed on cheap paper and with charming woodcut illustrations. One of the best known printers of such chapbooks was John Harkness of Preston, who was in business as a printer from the 1840s. His text, however, had some of the lines misplaced and the following script, whilst similar to Harkness', is based on a version printed by Joseph Wrigley of Manchester, *c*.1840.

## The **Peace Egg**

**Act 1** *(Enter Actors)*

*Fool*
Room, room, Brave gallants, give us room to sport,
For in this room we wish for to resort,
Resort, and to repeat to you our merry rhyme,
For remember, good sirs, this is Christmas time.
The time to cut up goose-pies now doth appear,
So we are come to act our merry Christmas here.
At the sound of the trumpet, and the beat of the drum,
Make room, brave gentlemen, and let our actors come.
We are the merry actors that traverse the street
We are the merry actors that fight for our meat;
We are the merry actors that show pleasant play;
Step in, St. George, thou champion, and clear the way.

*(Enter St. George)*
I am St. George, who from old England sprung,
My famous name throughout the world hath rung.
Many bloody deeds and wonders have I made known,
And made the tyrants tremble on their throne.
I followed a fair lady to a giants gate,
Confined in dungeon deep to meet her fate;
Then I resolved, with true knight-errantry,
To burst the door, and set the prisoner free.

When a giant almost struck me dead,
But by my valour I cut off his head.
I've searched the world all round and round,
But a man to equal me I never found.

*[Enter Slasher to St. George.]*
*Slasher*
I am a valiant soldier, and Slasher is my name,
With sword and buckler by my side I hope to win the game;
And for to fight with me I see thou are not able;
So with my trusty broad-sword I soon will thee disable.

| | |
|---|---|
| *St. George* | Disable! disable! it lies not in thy power; |
| | For with my glittering sword & spear I soon will thee devour. |

Stand off! Slasher! let no more be said,
For if I draw my sword, I'm sure to break thy head.

| | |
|---|---|
| *Slasher* | How can'st thou break my head? |
| | Since it is made of iron, |
| | And my body's made of steel, |
| | My hands and feet of knuckle bone, |
| | I challenge thee to field. |

*(They fight and Slasher is wounded. Exit St. George. Enter Fool)*

| | |
|---|---|
| *Fool* | Alas! alas! My chiefest son is slain, |
| | What must I do to raise him up again? |
| | Here he lies in the presence of you all; |
| | I'll lovingly for a doctor call. |
| | *(Aloud)* A doctor! A doctor! ten pounds for a doctor! |
| | I'll go and fetch a doctor, *(turns to go)* |

*Derbyshire Plough Play*

*(Enter Doctor)*

| | |
|---|---|
| *Doctor* | Here am I. |
| *Fool* | Are you the Doctor. |
| *Doctor* | Yes; that you may plainly see, by my art and activity. |
| *Fool* | Well, What's your fee to cure this man? |
| *Doctor* | Ten pounds is my fee: but Jack,<br>if thou be an honest man, I'll only take five off thee. |
| *Fool [aside]* | You'll be wondrous cunning if you get any.<br>Well, how far have you travelled in doctrineship? |
| *Doctor* | From Italy, Titaly, High Germany, France, and Spain;<br>And now am returned to cure the diseases in Old<br>England again. |
| *Fool* | So far, and no further. |
| *Doctor* | Oh yes! A great deal further. |
| *Fool* | How far? |
| *Doctor* | From the fireside, cupboard, upstairs and into bed. |
| *Fool* | What diseases can you cure? |
| *Doctor* | All sorts. |
| *Fool* | What's all sorts? |
| *Doctor* | The itch, the pitch, the palsy, & the gout.<br>If a man gets nineteen devils in his skull,<br>I'll cast twenty of them out.<br>I have in my pockets crutches for lame ducks, spectacles for<br>blind humble bees, packsaddles and panniers for<br>grasshoppers, and plaisters for broken-backed mice. I cured<br>Sir Harry of a nang-nail, almost fifty-five yards long, surely I<br>can cure this poor man.- Here, Jack; take a little out of my<br>bottle, and let it run down thy throttle; if thou be not quite<br>slain, rise, Jack, and fight again. |
| *Slasher* (rises) | O, my back! |
| *Fool* | What's amiss with thy back? |

| Slasher | My back it is wounded, |
|---|---|
| | And my heart is confounded, |
| | To be struck out of seven senses into four-score; |
| | The like was never seen in old England before! |

*(Enter St. George).*

O hark! St. George, I hear the silver trumpet sound,
That summons us from off this bloody ground;
Down yonder is the way. (*pointing*)
Farewell, St. George, we can no longer stay.

*(Exit Slasher, Doctor, and Fool)*

## Act 2

| St. George | I am St. George, that noble champion bold; |
|---|---|
| | And with my trusty sword I won ten thousand pounds in gold; |
| | 'Twas I that fought the fiery dragon, and brought him to the slaughter, |
| | And by those means I won the King of Egypt's daughter. |

*(Enter Prince of Paradine)*

| Prince | I am Black Prince of Paradine, born of high renown; |
|---|---|
| | Soon I will fetch St. George's lofty courage down! |
| | Before St. George shall be received by me, |
| | St. George shall die to all eternity. |
| St. George | Stand off, thou black Morocco dog, |
| | Or by my sword thou'lt die; |
| | I'll pierce thy body full of holes, |
| | And make thy buttons fly. |
| Prince | Draw out thy sword and slay, |
| | Pull out thy purse and pay, |
| | For I will have a recompense, |
| | Before I go away. |
| St. George | Now, Prince of Paradine, where have you been, |
| | And what fine sights pray have you seen: |
| | Do'st think that no man of thy age, |
| | Dares such a black as thee engage? |
| | Lay down thy sword, take up to me a spear, |
| | And then I'll fight thee without dread or fear. |

*(They fight and Prince of Paradine is slain.*

| *St. George* | Now Prince of Paradine is dead,<br>And all his joys entirely fled,<br>Take him and give him to the flies,<br>Let him no more come near my eyes. |

*(Enter King of Egypt)*

| *King* | I am the King of Egypt, as plainly doth appear,<br>I'm come to seek my son, my son and only heir. |

| *St. George* | He is slain. |

| *King* | Who did him slay, who did him kill,<br>And on the ground his precious blood did spill? |

| *St. George* | I did him slay, I did him kill,<br>And on the ground his precious blood did spill.<br>Please you, my liege, my honour to maintain,<br>Had you been there, you might have fared the same. |

| *King* | Cursed Christian! What is this thou'st done?<br>Thou has ruined me, and slain my only son. |

| *St. George* | He gave me a challenge, why should I it deny?<br>How high he was, but see how low he lies. |

| *King*<br><br>*(Enter Hector)* | O Hector! Hector! help me with speed,<br>For in my life I never stood more in need.<br>And stand not there with sword in hand,<br>But rise and fight at my command. |

| *Hector* | Yes, yes, my liege, I will obey;<br>And by my sword I hope to win the day.<br>If that be he who doth stand there,<br>That slew my master's son and heir,<br>If he be sprung from royal blood,<br>I'll make it run like Noah's flood, |

| *St. George* | Hold Hector! do not be so hot,<br>For here thou knowest not who thou'st got,<br>For I can tame thee of thy pride,<br>And lay thine anger, too, aside;<br>Inch thee, and cut thee as small as flies,<br>And send thee over the sea, to make mince pies.<br>Mince pies hot, and mince pies cold,<br>I'll send thee to Black Sam before thou't three days old. |

| *Hector* | How canst thou tame me of my pride,<br>And lay mine anger, too, aside, |

Inch me, and cut me as small as flies,
Send me over the sea to make mince pies?
Mince pies hot, and mince pies cold,
How canst thou send me to Black Sam before I'm three days old?
Since my head is made of iron, My body's made of steel,
My hands and feet of knuckle bone - I challenge thee to field.

*(They fight and Hector is wounded.)*

I am a valiant knight, and Hector is my name,
Many bloody battles have I fought and always won the same;
But from St. George I received this bloody wound.

*(A trumpet sounds)*

Hark! hark! I hear the silver trumpet sound;
Down yonder is the way,          *(pointing)*
Farewell, St. George, I can no longer stay.    *(Exit)*

*(Enter Fool to St. George)*

St. George      Here comes from post, old Bold Ben.

Fool            Why, master, did I ever take you to be my friend?

St. George      Why, Jack, did I ever do thee any harm?

Fool            Thou proud, saucy coxcomb, begone!

St. George      A coxcomb! I defy that name;
                With a sword thou ought to be stabbed for the same.

Fool            To be stabbed is the least I fear;
                Appoint your time and place, I'll meet you there.

St. George      I'll cross the water, at the hour of five
                And meet you there, Sir, if I be alive.    *(Exit)*

*(Enter Beelzebub)*

Here come I, Beelzebub, and over my shoulders I carry my club,
And in my hand a dripping pan, and I think myself a jolly old man,
And if you don't believe what I say,
Enter in Devil-doubt and clear the way.

*(Enter Devil Doubt)*

Here come I, little Devil Doubt, if you do not give me money I'll sweep you all out.
Money I want and money I crave; if you don't give me money, I'll sweep you all to the grave.

# 8  Tarvin Souling Play

This Souling play text was written out for Mrs K Synge by Joe Neild in c.1950. The play was performed in Tarvin and district, Cheshire, up to about 1920.

*Characters in order of appearance:*
**Open Doors** Usually the most daring of the cast.
**King George (or St George)** The tallest and the smartest.
**Turkish Knight** Smaller than King George.
**Old Woman** One with a high pitched voice.
**Doctor Brown** Well dressed & 'posh'
**Beelzebub** Generally the boss & carried the money collected.

*Open Doors also takes the part of the Old Horse's hind legs, the head being made from two brush heads, with bristles burnt off and ears added, and painted to look rather fearsome. A leather hinge joins the two together and it opens and shuts by the pulling of a string attached. An old bag or cloth covers "Open Doors".*

*(The characters assemble at their first call and all start to sing)*
We are two or three hearty lads and we're all in one mind.
We have all come a Souling good nature to find
But it's all we are Souling for is your shilling and your pence.
Step down in your cellar and see what you will find,
You will find all sorts of brandy and all sorts of wine.
But it's all we are Souling for is your shillings and your pence.

*'Open Doors' then knocks and enters saying:*
Please open these doors and let all our brave and gallant actors in
For we're all inclined to see King George win.
Room, room, gallant room, room we do require,
And if you can't believe these words I say
Step in King George and show thy face like fire.

*Enter King George*
In steps I king George the man of courage bold,
With my broad shield and sword I won 10, 000 pound in gold.
I slayed the fiery dragon and led him to the slaughter,
And by these very same means I won the king of Egypt's daughter.
If any man dare stand before me this night
I will hack him and smash him and send him
to Turkey land to be made into mince pies.

*Enter Turkish Knight*

In steps I the Turkish Knight,
I've come all the way from Turkey land to fight.
I'll fight thee King George, thou man of courage bold,
If thy blood be too hot, I'll quickly make it cold.

King George   Ah, ah, my little fellow, thou talkest very bold,
Thou talkest like one of these Turkish Knights as I have oft
been told.
Draw out thy purse and pay, Draw out thy sword and slay,
For I will have satisfaction on thee before thou goest away.

Turkish Knight   Satisfaction, no satisfaction on me for my head is made
of iron,
My body is made of steel, my arms and legs are made of
knuckle bone,
So how can'st thou kill me?

King George   Stand back thou black morroccodile.

Turkish Knight   Oh King George, King George, pardon me and I will
be thy slave forever.

King George   Pardon! I never pardon a Turkish Knight. Prepare.

*King George and Turkish Knight do battle and the Turkish Knight falls mortally
wounded. In rushes the 'Old Woman' saying:*
Oh, King George, King George, what has't thou done,
Thou has't killed and slain my only son, my only heir.
How can'st thou stand to see him bleeding there.

King George   Why he challenged me out to fight so why should I deny?

Old Woman   Are there any doctors to be found?

*Enter Dr Brown*
Yes. In steps I Dr Brown, the finest quack doctor
in all this town.
Here Jack take three drops of this down thy
thripple thropple.

Turkish Knight   Oh my back.

Old Woman   What ails thy back my son?

Turkish Knight   My back is wounded and my heart is confounded,
He has knocked me into ten score twenty.

| | |
|---|---|
| *Dr. Brown* | Oh Patsy, Patsy, I quite forgot. I've given him the wrong medicine.<br>I have a little bottle in my topside, middleside, inside, outside waistcoat pocket<br>That my Uncle Aunt Jane sent me form Spain<br>To raise dead men to life again.<br>Here Jack take three drops of this down thy thripple-thropple<br>And rise up and fight the battle. |
| *Old Woman* | How camest thou to be a doctor? |
| *Dr. Brown* | By my travels. |
| *Old Woman* | What are thy travels? |
| *Dr. Brown* | Up hills and mountains where thou couldn't get. |
| *Old Woman* | How did you get up there? |
| *Dr. Brown* | Cut my arms and legs off and threw myself up there. |
| *Old Woman* | What did you see up there? |
| *Dr. Brown* | I saw two dead men fighting,<br>Two blind men seeing fair play,<br>Two men without arms or legs<br>Running for the bobby. |
| *Old Woman* | Is that all? |
| *Dr. Brown* | Yes, plenty for a doctor to know<br>And if you don't believe these words I say,<br>Step in Beehelzebub and clear the way. |

*Enter Beehelzebub with Old Horse - carrying a club and dripping pan.*
In steps I Beehelzebub. On my shoulder I carry a club,
In my hand a dripping tin. Rin-tin-tin.
A drop more water would dry the kettle dry, Sally.
Rin-tin-tin.
This Old Horse he's fat in front, he's fat behind,
He's all oe'r except his tail and that's made of suet.
That's the stuff for making these farmhouse lads and
wenches suet dumplings.
Come up Dick, whoa! *(Horse winches)*
This Old Horse he's got an eye like a hawk; a neck like a
swan

And a foot like a paver's jammack and a tail like a tachinend.
Come up Dick, whoa! *(Horse winches)*

Now if you want to know anything more about this Old
Horse
You must go to the Manchester and Liverpool Grid Iron
Company where there is no writing at all.
This Old Horse, he's travelled high, he's travelled low,
He's travelled through the hail, rain, frost and snow.
He's travelled through streets paved with pancakes
And houses thatched with dumplings.
With little pigs running about with knives and forks
stuck in their backs crying out 'who'll eat me, who'll eat
me?'
This poor Old Horse was coming down Mouldsworth Hill the
other day with a load of 'Fir Bobs' and one fell off and Dick
kicked and kicked the front, back of the cart out.
So will you please give us a copper or two to buy Dick a
new cart with.

*Beehelzebub then proceeds to collect in the dripping tin saying:*
Christmas is coming and the goose is getting fat,
Will you please to put something in the old man's hat.
If you haven't got a penny, a halfpenny will do,
If you haven't got a halfpenny God Bless You.

*Just before leaving all sing :*
And the next that steps in is Bold William you see,
He's a gallant old fellow in every degree.
Fol - di - diddle - I - di - di. Fol - di - diddle - I - di - di.

# 9 A Robin Hood Play

This version is adapted from a play printed in *The Mummers Play* by
R.J.E.Tiddy (1923). The play was written down in 1868 from John
Couling, a member of an old family in Kempsford, Gloucestershire. The
mummers' costume was described as hats of paper decorated with
plumes or coloured ribbons hanging down and each man carried a
sword. The character Tom Pinny, who also played Father Christmas,
wore a mask leaving part of his face bare, which was painted red! He
wore a fool's cap and carried an instrument which he pretended to play
as a fiddle. He was also made to appear a hunchback with straw stuffed
up inside his coat and he carried a can to collect money. These
mummers went out to the large houses at Christmas time, knocked on
the door and requested "Please let the mummers act." The performers
would walk round and round with the audience surrounding them.

## The **play**

*Arthur Abland (a tanner)*

    A room a room brave gallants all
    Please give me room to rhyme
    This merry, merry Christmas time
    Activity of youth and activity of age
    Such life was never seen upon the stage

    As I was a walking one Summer's morning
    Through the forest merry greenwood
    To view the red deer
    Then I saw bold Robin Hood.

*(Enter Robin Hood)*

    As soon as Robin Hood did me spy
    Some sport he thought to make
    He bid me fan he bid me stand
    And he bid me thus for to spake.

*Robin*

    Who art thou bold fellow,
    Who comes so boldly here
    Now to be brief thou looks a thief
    Come to steal the King's deer.
    I'm the keeper over this forest
    And the King put me in trust
    To mind the red deer
    That run here and run there.
    So stop you Good fellow I must

*Arthur*

    If you are keeper over this forest

And has any great command
I don't care a fig for you looking so big
So mind yourself where you can.

Robin      Let us measure staves, bold fellow
Before we begin our play
I won't have my staff half a foot longer than thine
Else that will come to foul play

Arthur     My staff is eight-foot and a half
And growed straight on a tree
An eight-foot staff will knock down a castle
And I'm sure it will knock down thee

(they fight)

Robin      Oh, hold our hands,
Oh, hold our hands
And let our quarrels fall
We shall beat our bones all to a meat
And get no where at all.
If you will leave your tanning trade
And bide in greenwood with me,
My name's Robin Hood andI swear by the wood
I will give you both gold and fee.

Enter Little John
What is the matter master
I pray you to me tell
You stand with your staff all in your hand
I'm afraid things aren't too well

Robin      The man that bid me stand
Is the tanner by my side;
He's a bonny blade
And a master by trade
And he swears he'll tan my hide.

Little John   If you be so big and stout
You and I will have a bout
(They fight and Little John knocks down Arthur)

Robin      A thousand pounds I'll freely give
If Arthur Abland's life we can save.

Enter Doctor (on Tom Pinny's back)
Doctor     Hold my horse, Jack.

| | |
|---|---|
| *Tom Pinny* | Yes Sir, I've got him fast by the tail |
| *Doctor* | Rack him up with a faggot and<br>Give him a bucket of ashes to drink. |
| *Doctor (rattling a pillbox)* | See Sirs, here comes the Noble doctor<br>Both stout and good<br>And with my hand and my skill<br>I will stop his blood. |
| *Robin* | What country do you come from? |
| *Doctor* | From Italy, Tittaly, France and Spain<br>And then twice round the world again |
| *Robin* | What can you cure? |
| *Doctor* | All sorts of diseases - just what the pill pleases.<br>The heart corn and smart corn'<br>The itch, the snitch, the palsy and the gout<br>The pain within and the pains without |
| *Robin* | What else can you cure? |
| *Doctor* | Horses, cows, sheep and pigs<br>And so walk in Master Clever Legs. |
| *Tom Pinny (from without)* | What's the matter with my legs more than your own? |
| *Doctor* | Walk in Tom Pinny |
| *Tom Pinny* | Tom Pinny's not my name |
| *Doctor* | What is your name? |
| *Tom Pinny* | Master Tom Pinny, a man of great fame<br>Doesn't thou know my name?<br>Here come I, as can't be hit<br>With my great head and my little wit<br>My head's so big and my wit's so small<br>I've come to try to please you all |
| *Robin* | What can you cure? |
| *Tom Pinny* | A magpie with the tooth ache. |
| *Robin* | How do you do that? |

*Marshfield Paper Boys, Gloucestershire*

| | |
|---|---|
| *Tom Pinny* | Cut off his head and throw his body into a ditch. |
| *Robin* | What country do you come from? |
| *Tom Pinny* | I come from the country where they knits horses shoes<br>And spins steel iron bars<br>And thatches pigsties with pancakes.<br>Have you got any? |
| *Doctor* | Bellows, if you please, missus! |

*(Takes a pair of bellows and blows into Arthur's mouth.)*
> Rise up bold Arthur Abland and
> Give the Ladies and Gentlemen a dance before
> you go away

*(They all dance and Tom Pinny sings to his fiddle)*
> So here I am, a rub a dub, dub,
> On my shoulder I carries my club
> In my hand an empty can
> Don't you think I'm a jolly old man.
> Now my boys we'll dance apace
> Hump back and hairy wig
> Now me boys, we'll dance a jig

# 10 Pace-egging song (Lancashire)

From the singing of Mrs. Emma Vickers of Burscough, Lancashire, who revived a version of the play in the village and knew two versions of the song.

There's one or two jolly lads all in one mind,
We've come a-pace-egging, if you will provide,
With your eggs and strong beer we'll come no more here,
Until the next year at pace-egging time.
*Chorus:*
Fol the diddle ol aye day, Fol the diddle ol aye day.

The next that comes in is our bold British tar,
He sailed with Lord Nelson all during the war,
But now he's come back Old England to view,
He's come a-pace-egging with our jovial crew.
*Chorus.*

The next that comes in is our lady so gay,
And from her own country she has run away,
On her arm is a basket, your eggs to put in,
And all her delight is in drinking neat gin.
*Chorus.*

The next that comes in is our Tosspot, you see,
He's a valiant old man in every degree,
He's a valiant old man and he wears a straw tail,
And all he delights in is drinking mulled ale.
*Chorus.*

Our time is so short, our journey so long,
We hope you'll excuse us for this very short song,
Put your hand in your pocket and pull out your purse,
And give us a trifle, you'll never be no worse.
*Chorus.*

# Acknowledgments

*Photographs by Doc Rowe: on pages 20, 23, 28, 53 (bottom), 54, 61 (bottom), 62, 64, 70, 72 (top), 81, 114. Also all pictures in the colour section, back cover (top and bottom right), front cover and distribution map on page 29.*

*Illustrations and photographs from Doc Rowe Collection: on pages 2, 4, 7, 8, 10, 14, 26, 32, 45, 53 (top), 61 (top), 66, 72 (bottom), 82, 90, 96, 103 and 118.*

*Photographs on back cover (left) by Sir Benjamin Stone, page 10 by George Long and page 24 from Ordish Collection (The Folklore Society).*

Shrewton, Wiltshire, 1936